Ethics of Engagement in Research Practices

This book elaborates on the concept of response-ability. Although the notion is becoming popular in organization and management studies to talk about the ethical dimension of academic practices and research work, it has been formulated outside this discipline with Joan Tronto, Donna Haraway, Vinciane Despret, and Karen Barad as key authors. This book honors the foundational contribution of these scholars and their legacy.

This book adopts a feminist posthumanist definition of response-ability as an iterative and emergent process that unfolds within embodied relations and through academic practices. A response-able academic practice intertwines personal reflexivity and critical analysis of the politics underlying our ways of knowing and doing in academia. Furthermore, a response-able approach requires us, as researchers, to pay attention to the consequences of our research practices through which multiple encounters are made possible (or impossible).

By offering empirical examples and theoretical elaborations, this book invites students, researchers, and practitioners to find ways of embodying response-ability when generating knowledge.

Michela Cozza is an Associate Professor at the Department of Organization and Management at Mälardalen University, Sweden. Her research interests focus on the relationships between social and material aspects of organizational practices. She takes a practice-based approach and leverages a science and technology studies perspective to understand issues related to technology's role in embodied practices of care and technological interventions. She is a member of several research networks, scientific associations, and editorial boards.

Anna Carreri is an Assistant Professor (tenure track) of Sociology of Work and Organization at the Department of Human Sciences of the University of Verona, Italy. She is a scientific coordinator and co-founder of the Research Centre RE-WOrk: REsearching for REmaking Work and Organizing at the same university. She is affiliated with the School of Social Sciences at Hasselt University, Belgium. Her research is mainly conducted through qualitative methods, from an intersectional and critical perspective. Her current research is focused on gender inequalities in academic careers and the quality of working life in relation to 'new' forms of work and organizing enabled by technology.

Barbara Poggio is the Vice-Rector for Equality and Diversity at the University of Trento, Italy. She is a Full Professor of Sociology of Work and Organization at the Department of Sociology and Social Research at the same university. She carried out several international studies and research in the field of gender studies (gender cultures and practices in organizations, gender and entrepreneurship, gender and science), workforce diversity, work precariousness, and work-life balance. She is a member of several national and international editorial boards.

Routledge Focus on Women Writers in Management and Organization Studies

Series Note

Given that women and men have always engaged in and thought about organizing, why is it that core management texts are dominated by the writing of men? This series redresses the neglect of women in organization thought and practice and highlights their contributions. Through a selection of carefully curated short-form books, it covers major themes such as structure, rationality, managing, leading, culture, power, ethics, diversity and sustainability; and also attends to contemporary debates surrounding performativity, the body, emotion, materiality and postcoloniality. Individually, each book provides stand-alone coverage of a key sub-area within organization studies, with a contextual series introduction written by the editors. Collectively, the titles in the series give a global overview of how women have shaped organizational thought.

Routledge Focus on Women Writers in Management and Organization Studies will be relevant to students and researchers across business and management, organizational studies, critical management studies, gender studies and sociology.

Morality, Ethics and Responsibility in Organization and Management
Edited by Robert McMurray and Alison Pullen

Affect in Organization and Management
Edited by Carolyn Hunter and Nina Kivinen

Postcolonial Feminism in Management and Organization Studies
Critical Perspectives from India, Pakistan and Bangladesh
Edited by Vijayta Doshi

Ethics of Engagement in Research Practices
Response-ability in Organization and Management
Edited by Michela Cozza, Anna Carreri, and Barbara Poggio

For more information about this series, please visit: www.routledge.com/Routledge-Focus-on-Women-Writers-in-Organization-Studies/book-series/RFWWOS

Ethics of Engagement in Research Practices

Response-ability in Organization and Management

Edited by
Michela Cozza, Anna Carreri, and Barbara Poggio

NEW YORK AND LONDON

First published 2025
by Routledge
605 Third Avenue, New York, NY 10158

and by Routledge
4 Park Square, Milton Park, Abingdon, Oxon, OX14 4RN

Routledge is an imprint of the Taylor & Francis Group, an informa business

Library of Congress Cataloging-in-Publication Data
Names: Cozza, Michela, editor. | Carreri, Anna, editor. | Poggio, Barbara, 1967– editor.
Title: Ethics of engagement in research practices : response-ability in organization and management / edited by Michela Cozza, Anna Carreri, and Barbara Poggio.
Description: New York, NY : Routledge, 2025. | Series: Routledge focus on women writers in organization studies | Includes bibliographical references and index.
Identifiers: LCCN 2024033008 | ISBN 9781032587240 (hardback) | ISBN 9781032589916 (paperback) | ISBN 9781003452485 (ebook)
Subjects: LCSH: Social sciences—Research—Moral and ethical aspects. | Posthumanism.
Classification: LCC H62 .E779 2025 | DDC 001.4/2—dc23/eng/20240809
LC record available at https://lccn.loc.gov/2024033008

ISBN: 978-1-032-58724-0 (hbk)
ISBN: 978-1-032-58991-6 (pbk)
ISBN: 978-1-003-45248-5 (ebk)

DOI: 10.4324/9781003452485

Typeset in Times New Roman
by codeMantra

Contents

Contributors

Anna Carreri is an Assistant Professor (tenure track) of Sociology of Work and Organization at the Department of Human Sciences at the University of Verona, Italy.

Alessia Contu is a Professor of Management at the University of Massachusetts Boston, USA.

Michela Cozza is an Associate Professor in Business Administration at the Department of Organization and Management at Mälardalen University, Sweden.

Marcelo de Souza Bispo is an Associate Professor of Management and Sociology at Federal University of Paraiba, Brazil.

Leni Grünbaum is a doctoral researcher at the Aalto University School of Business, Espoo, Finland.

Emmanouela Mandalaki is an Associate Professor of Organizations at NEOMA Business School, France.

Laura Lucia Parolin is an Associate Professor of Organizational Communication at the University of Southern Denmark, Denmark.

Carmen Pellegrinelli, PhD in Social Science at the University of Lapland, Finland, is a research collaborator at the University of Trento, Italy, and a theatre playwright and director.

Barbara Poggio is a Professor of Sociology of Work and Organization at the Department of Sociology and Social Research at the University of Trento, Italy.

Jared M. Poole is an Assistant Professor of Management at the University of Massachusetts Boston, USA.

Maureen A. Scully is a Professor of Management at the University of Massachusetts Boston, USA.

Alice Wickström is a postdoctoral researcher at the School of Business, Economics and Law at the University of Gothenburg, Sweden.

1 Introduction. Ethics of Engagement in Research Practices

Response-ability in Organization and Management

Michela Cozza, Anna Carreri, and Barbara Poggio

A Cartographic Reading of 'Response-ability'

Cartography or mapmaking is the study and practice of making maps. It combines science, esthetics, and technique to visualize and communicate spatial data effectively. The word 'cartography' refers to both a multifaceted discipline – combining geography, design, and technology – and a tool for navigating familiar or uncharted territories. It is especially useful for those who move across variegated landscapes and different locations. Metaphorically, cartography can fulfill a methodological function in knowledge-making practices to creatively guide researchers through complex material-discursive webs of power that are operational in and immanent to the production and circulation of knowledge (Braidotti 2019). From this perspective, using cartography requires an ethical sensibility to the multiple encounters that are enabled by nomadic research and situated in political arenas (Antoni and Beer 2023). A cartographic approach relies on *response-ability*, which is the capacity to respond to others and make each other capable of responding along margins of hope for new or alternative horizons of care and epistemic plurality (i.e., affirmative ethics) while foregrounding embodied and embedded conditions of oppression and subjection.

Response-ability is the foundational concept of this book. It is read through the cartographic lens of feminist posthumanism to encourage a renewal of subjectivities and practices in management and organization studies (MOS). Response-ability lies in the possibility of an upheaval of the disciplinary and methodological boundaries that prevent or discourage researchers from exploring unfamiliar ontologies and epistemologies and attuning to their subjects/objects of study (Rogowska-Stangret 2020). To appreciate the concept of 'response-ability' in this first section, we suggest a cartographic reading of its origins and subsequent uses.

DOI: 10.4324/9781003452485-1

The origins of the concept 'response-ability' lie in fields outside MOS, with Joan Tronto (1993, 2012, 2015, 2020), Donna Haraway (2008, 2016), Vinciane Despret (2004, 2008, 2013, 2020), and Karen Barad (2007, 2019) as key figures in the development of the concept. It gained traction in MOS (e.g., Bruzzone 2021; Cozza and Gherardi 2023; Gherardi and Laasch 2022) through theoretical exploration and onto-epistemological experimentation, though not without the difficulty inherent in a nomadic inquiry attuned to the instability and unpredictability of the world. What we present here is a basic map generated by the thinking of scholars who have greatly contributed to the theorization of what response-ability is, does, and offers to MOS scholars. However, it is not an ordinary map in that it does not represent a single trajectory. Rather, it represents a kind of rhizomatic thinking through different lines of analysis of response-ability (Lenz Taguchi 2013). Rhizomatic thinking enables us as researchers to think about "connections rather than oppositions, movement rather than categorization, and becoming rather than being" (St Pierre 2013, 653). It is based on a different kind of ethics, which is affirmative in that it requires "a belief in this world" (Deleuze and Guattari 1994, 92) and response-ability to make another world (or worlds) possible.

We should start by pointing out that responsibility (accountability) and response-ability (ability to respond) are two distinct concepts, though both terms are interconnected and predicated on a relational ontology according to which the world is an assemblage of inextricably entangled entities (Bozalek 2020). "Entanglements are not intertwinings of separate entities, but rather irreducible *relations of responsibility* (…) Entanglements are *relations of obligation*" (Barad 2010, 265; emphasis added). Still, responsibility and response-ability relate to different practices and sensibilities.

> According to care ethicists, *responsibility* is about acting on the need for care *once it has been identified*. For others, mainly posthumanists and feminist new materialists, responsibility is equated with accountability for marks on bodies (…) *Response-ability* is *also* about *inviting and enabling a response* in attunement with the specificity of the situation, and in so doing, rendering the involved parties capable.
>
> (Bozalek and Zembylas 2023, 8–9; emphasis added)

Hence, we can say that response-ability "actualises responsibility through engagements and interventions" (Rogowska-Stangret 2020, 17) that allow living beings and other entities to enter deep relations of caring proximity (Carstens 2020).

Joan C. Tronto (1993), in defining an ethics of care, introduces four elements: attentiveness, responsibility, competence, and responsiveness. The latter is similar to the notion of response-ability in that it requires that we – as humans and, specifically, as researchers – remain alert to possibilities of dependence *and* independence, autonomy, *and* vulnerability emerging in relationships. Responsiveness suggests a different way to understand the needs of others *as expressed by the others,* rather than as understood by putting ourselves into their position. It is a posture far removed from 'empowering' or 'giving voice,' where both concepts suggest a kind of action carried out from within a system of dominance and assimilation (Higgins 2021) and both terms are reminiscent of a colonizer narrative. "In the context of the academy, responsibility with an inventive rupture implies, first and foremost, the ability of interrupting the self, of moving beyond the 'I' as the [exclusive] ethical subject" (Kuokkanen 2010, 65).

Echoing Karen Barad (2012), a response-able research apparatus is not meant to enable us as researchers to *react* differently to the world – as if the researcher is an external observer – but rather to allow us *to stay in* the world, to be and become differently in intra-action *with* it, and to learn how to 'touch' the other by being aware that "[a]ll touching entails an infinite alterity so that touching the other is touching all others, including the 'self'" (Barad 2019, 532). It can be a material or a discursive touch, like a welcoming or dismissive gesture, an indifferent or inquisitive look, or an awkward or comfortable silence. In research, all forms of touching have different meanings to different actors and contribute to agential cuts (Barad 2007), or doings, that enact what matters and what is excluded from mattering (Bozalek and Fullagar 2022). The research apparatus is thus built on practices that enable an articulation of the world through bodies that are entangled and co-constitute knowledge, generating possibilities and impossibilities, inclusion and exclusion. A response-able research practice sees "epistemic plurality as gift rather than a lack that requires repair" (Higgins 2021, vii) through the authority of *S*cience.

Donna Haraway (1988, 582) has pointed out that to be response-able in our research practices, "[w]e need to learn in our bodies" and argue "for the view from a body, always a complex, contradictory, structuring, and structured body, versus the view from above, from nowhere, from simplicity" (589). Producing knowledge is neither neutral nor innocent, and a response-able practice asks us as researchers to deal with the fact that "[w]e cannot play the innocent and produce conceptual ideals warranting our innocence. Accepting that we are in the mud means that living is dangerous, and thinking is dangerous" (Savransky and Stengers 2018, 135). Research requires daring and openness to unexpected collaborations and combinations "in hot compost piles" (Haraway 2016, 4). Despite centuries of human (Western) exceptionalism, humans can only pretend to be autonomous, independent, and disentangled from nonhumans and more-than-humans, while in fact "[w]e are at stake to each other" (55) because "nothing is really autopoietic or self-organizing" (58). Researchers make no exception. Accordingly, rather than framing research as a unilateral mode of organizing knowledge from above or from outside, we could conceptualize it as 'sympoiesis,' which means 'making with' from within, "always in the midst" (Manning 2016, 37), in composition with others. Conceiving of research as sympoietic enhances response-ability in world-making practices and attunes them with affective intensities – feeling, sensation, and desire – circulating in research intra-actions.

Vinciane Despret emphasizes that "[m]eanings are constructed in a constant movement of *attunement*" (2008, 125; emphasis in original) and "subjectivities overlap, are transformed, actualized and extended to the subjectivity of the other" (129). In a world that is "[s]lippery, indistinct, elusive, complex, diffuse, messy, textured, vague, unspecific, confused, disordered, emotional, painful, pleasurable, hopeful, horrific, lost, redeemed, visionary, angelic, demonic, mundane, intuitive, sliding and unpredictable" (Law 2004, 6), engaging in a response-able research practice entails appreciating it as embodied and situated. Scholars who invest in establishing a relationship with their 'object' of study are often dismissed as unscientific or untrustworthy. Despret (2013, 52–53, emphasis in original) reminds us that a disembodied research practice

> is a means to preclude (to prevent or to avoid) the always possible reciprocity of the encounter – as we shall see, 'having a body' discloses and renders perceptible the very existence of this reciprocity: moreover, it *is* the actual condition of its existence.

However, simply acknowledging that we are entangled with others in research practices is insufficient to enact response-ability. It demands attentiveness (Tronto 1993 [2009]) and the ability to notice and act with the latencies and diversities of living experience (Simpson and Revsbæk 2022). Despret and Meuret (2016, 26–27; emphasis in original) state that attentiveness, or noticing, "requires us to expand the scope of obligations," to compromise ourselves or – following Stengers (Stengers, Massumi and Manning 2009, n.p.) – "[b]eing obligated by the situation, giving the situation the power to obligate you. And without guarantees." On the contrary, we add that the authority of *S*cience or methodological standardization is meant to 'protect' us as researchers from the troubles of making knowledge in the muddle of contemporary life, but, in doing so, it prevents us from becoming with the world we study. Attentiveness corresponds to what Anna Tsing (2015, 24) calls the "arts of noticing" or the ability to think relationally and "to appreciate the multiple temporal rhythms and trajectories of the assemblage." According to Tsing, noticing is not something that simply happens, it needs to be cultivated. It is

> both a practice of getting to know another in their intimate particularity (…) and, at the same time, a practice of learning how one might better respond to another, might work to cultivate worlds of mutual flourishing (…) In short, the arts of attentiveness remind us that knowing and living are deeply entangled and that paying attention can and should be the basis for crafting better possibilities for shared life.
>
> (Van Dooren, Kirksey and Münster 2016, 17)

In the following, we use the cartographic approach to elaborate on response-ability in academia by articulating some of the practices that enable responsiveness and attentiveness in MOS. We then move across and beyond academia, where MOS researchers encapsulate response-ability into world-making practices that shake the 'ivory tower.' We end this introduction by navigating through the chapters to provide an overview of the book.

Response-able Academic Practices

How should we challenge our ways of knowing in academia to build a space that fosters responsiveness and attentiveness in MOS? What are the needs of the individuals that higher education care for? What response-able practices can we enact in our intra-active relationships? These questions are the starting point for introducing an ethics of care within academia (Tronto 1993 [2009], 2015, 2020). As the chapters in this book clearly show, the way the above questions are addressed in practice is a matter for ethical and political discussion (Antoni and Beer 2023).

Response-ability, from a feminist posthumanist point of view, is an iterative and emergent process that unfolds within embodied relations and through our academic practices. It intertwines personal reflexivity and critical analysis of the politics underlying our ways of knowing and 'doing academia.' Enacting responsibility and response-ability in our academic practices is not an easy task. Yet, in this book, this task corresponds to a matter of concern that we – editors and authors – have *cared for* collectively by 'staying with the trouble' (Haraway 2016) that responsibility and response-ability bring to the fore. In other words, we have attempted to translate what is a matter of concern – such as the difficult task of accounting for our own responsibility as researchers while cultivating differential responsiveness in academic practices – into a matter of care that affects our being and doing in academia and, more broadly, our connection to the world we inhabit. Importantly, it is a concern that asks for caring about the future of academia and the 'peripheral' and overlapping world. With this book, we want to highlight and strengthen the connections between ethics and politics in, across, and around different organizations, including academia (Pullen and Rhodes 2015). In pursuing this very aim, we recognize ourselves, albeit in different forms depending on our positionalities.

Making each other 'capable of responding' is a situated practice (Gherardi and Rodeschini 2016). Care itself is a situated knowing and a collective knowledgeable doing within an organization. The authors' common orientation to this matter of care leads us to take some risks and reconsider our ways of operating in our fieldwork by generating and sharing scientific knowledge in MOS, making its disciplinary boundaries porous, and foregrounding the possibilities for enacting response-able academic practices through intra-actions.

Barad's (2007) concept of intra-action is useful in acknowledging that while we carry out a variety of tasks – doing field research, teaching, and attending to our duties of care with students and communities we come in contact with, writing and talking about our research achievements – we are always in the midst (Manning 2016), imbued with, and immersed in relational intricacies with other humans, nonhumans, and more-than-humans. From this point of view, response-ability is a relational rather than individualistic accomplishment, always integral to the world's ongoing intra-active becoming (Barad 2010; Kuokkanen 2010; Higgins 2021). This feminist posthumanist view questions the vertical and unidirectional notion of expert knowledge transmitted to 'less knowledgeable others' and invites us – as researchers – to acknowledge the margins that we make and to decolonize our knowledge-making practices (Bozaleck and Zembylas 2017; Cozza and Gherardi 2023).

This decentralization greatly exposes us to vulnerability and dependence, but it is precisely in this vulnerability (Cano Abadía 2021) that a space of responsiveness can be created (Tronto 1993). Embracing connectedness in the encounter with multiple others implies welcoming the unexpected, the unknown, the tensions, and the contradictions that may arise, as well as the possibilities and opportunities that others may offer. Paradoxically (or perhaps not), it is precisely in a position of vulnerability and dependence that we can appreciate the collaborative meaning of doing scientific research while banishing a sense of alienation and exclusiveness (Alakavuklar, Dickson and Stablein 2017). The increasing standardization of academia, which largely influences an individual saying and doing, disempowers the social and political impact that our work may have on the larger community with which it engages. As highlighted by Putnam, Fairhurst, and Banghart (2016), there is a dialectic between organizational order and disorder, and this extends to academia. The power and performativity of tensions, contradictions, and dilemmas are constitutive of our everyday organizational life and we – who inhabit the academic system – cannot disregard them. While adherence to rigid researcher authority and research boundaries (for example, between different roles and stages of the fieldwork) may prevent the full engagement and contribution of multiple others, making room for shared responsiveness and fluid boundaries enables affective intensities to nourish our research experience and release its transformative potential.

Response-ability in our academic practices also demands that attentiveness is cultivated and that researchers stay attuned to others' embodied and situated experiences (Despret 2008). Response-able research does not happen by listening and observing others at a distance but rather by affectively attuning to them and putting ourselves in the condition of knowing how to listen, how to notice (Gherardi and Cozza 2022), how to touch and be touched, and how to be generous to such an extent that stories can be shared and bodies can be reciprocally seen and affected, including the researcher's body (Kaasila-Pakanen et al. 2024). Attentiveness is a mutual process of noticing what is significant for others (Tsing 2015) and provoking meaningful (bodily) responses of attunement. The relational ontology of 'becoming with others' underpins the practice of response-ability not only within the limited timeframe of a project but continually in everyday academic practice. Response-ability through attentiveness is thus a process of generating knowledge in posthumanist engagement with multiple others. It is a mode of passionate immersion (Van Dooren, Kirksey and Münster 2016) that enfolds and unfolds the here-now and there-then, and in which the binary inside/outside does not make sense as there is neither 'outside' (Higgins 2021) nor a clear caesura between internal stages of a research.

Experimental, embodied, immersive, creative, transformative, risk-taking, and response-able practices in academia require care for the involved actors. We can identify at least three intra-active domains of academic caring practices addressing different recipients in never-neutral but rather always-political arenas (Antoni and Beer 2023). These refer to the participants in the fieldwork (caring research practices), peers (caring disciplinary practices), and students (caring pedagogical practices).

Caring field*work* requires attentiveness to interrogate prescriptive patterns and the establishment of artificial boundaries to order research stages (temporal linear boundaries) and keep 'clean' roles and scripts (distributive spatial boundaries). Response-ability entails 'getting our hands dirty' and creatively engaging with messy empirical material, troubling human needs, and unfathomable nonhuman alterity (Mazzei 2014). It also means making room for experimentation rather than disembodied research inquiries. Making each other capable of responding, while warding off the risk of subjecting others and ourselves to processes of epistemic oppression (Kaasila-Pakanen and Mandalaki 2023), requires an open dialogue across researchers' and multiple others' differences, without indulging in pre-assigned and constraining formats. Response-able academic practices enable mutual flourishing and allow different views to emerge as the research process unfolds (Antoni and Beer 2023). Accounting for the research results and how they have been achieved is a key aspect of response-ability toward research participants. It is an important form of caring *if* it is done by transcending a ritualistic execution (e.g., imposed by a project structure) and is not limited to academic events and activities (e.g., conferences) (Carreri 2022).

Response-ability in peer relationships within MOS (and beyond) relies on acknowledging that the norms of *scientific* writing, publishing, and peer review often ask us – as authors, editors or reviewers – to distance ourselves or peers from our/their body and the fleshy encounters we/they experience ('for the sake of objectivity') or even command to silence the recalcitrant liveness of those materials/'data' that (apparently) do not fit ('for the sake of methodological rigor') (Bozalek, Zembylas and Shefer 2019). However, no one is innocent. We all contribute to the inclusion/exclusion game played in the name of *S*cience, imposing rules and expectations of doing theory and managing 'data' in a certain way (Amrouche et al. 2018), reproducing a legitimized jargon or style, or fostering the reproduction of dominant narratives (Boncori 2022). Response-ability in MOS entails questioning how we – as authors – generate knowledge and how we let others do it: a case in point is the peer review process (Chapter 2 in this volume).

The academic community, however, is not limited to academicians. The enactment of response-ability entails care for students through a relational and emancipatory approach to teaching and learning (Cano Abadía 2021). In educational settings, embracing vulnerability and the unexpected as gifts may inspire a sense of responsive vigilance in students and teachers (Zembylas 2005). Response-able pedagogies "provide new ways of considering what matters and what is often excluded from mattering" (Bozaleck and Zembylas 2017, 64) across differences. In so doing, students and teachers develop individual awareness of the consequences of their own epistemic practices and, together, they can contribute to generating a more just knowledge (Contu 2020) (Chapter 3 in this volume).

All the above practices rely on an ethics of engagement and participative reciprocity across the narrow boundaries of academia. We elaborate on this ethical posture in the following section.

Response-ability as an Ethics of Engagement

The adoption of a response-able approach should not be limited to organizational or disciplinary boundaries (i.e., MOS) as it transcends them. Researchers' work often implies encounters with multiple others outside the academic environment. They can be human (as noted in the previous section: peers, students, and research participants), nonhuman actors (including the materiality of spaces and places), or more-than-humans (depending on the research topic, we could include animals and other living beings). Such encounters may occur while conducting research, in the managerial work that is often needed to accomplish academic and research activities, or even through researchers' public engagement and academic activism. In other words, a response-able approach requires us, as researchers, to pay attention not only to what is told through the results of research processes but also to what research practices, in their becoming, *do* to us and others by going through social worlds via different forms of actions and interventions. Moreover, a response-able approach always asks us to consider the ontological mutual entanglement and epistemological co-shaping enacted with others (Higgins 2021). Finally, it invites us to bear in mind that social processes are always situated in space and time and entail performative intra-actions in becoming with others.

The first type of engagement concerns the relationship with other actors or entities with whom the researchers may interact while conducting research. To expand on the previous section, research trajectories within organizations and workplaces are inevitably punctuated by encounters with various types of subjects, such as practitioners, managers, intermediaries, or other interlocutors, which is a necessary or strategic step in order to get access to the field. This step can also provide access to specific groups and contexts we intend to investigate for research purposes. These encounters happen through material-discursive practices enacted through rules, protocols, standards, artifacts, objects, technologies, and other (im)materialities populating the research setting. It is noteworthy that these heterogeneous elements are entangled and precariously connected as they 'become with' the research process itself. Hence, from an ethical viewpoint, the researcher can never be seen as an external and detached observer, but s/he is part of the unstable flux of practices under scrutiny, which s/he affects and by which s/he is affected. Gherardi (2019) suggests that adopting a response-able approach in organizational and management settings implies a sort of affective attunement that allows researchers to engage in an 'other-oriented' sense, a 'being with' others. This attunement goes beyond normative compliance with codes of conduct or institutional ethical principles, though it does not diminish their relevance. Rather than the mere enforcement of organizational rules and regulations, the ethics of engagement requires considering how to enable such an engagement and identifying its affective relations and embodied conditions. The flow of affective intensities that characterize all research encounters can influence the capacity of being and doing. Indeed, affect can facilitate or disturb the relationships and hinder the research process or open up new possibilities and avenues. Ethics of engagement invites us to acknowledge the im-possibilities arising in the research field and explore and learn from them, rather than simply reacting to them, perhaps in the name of a sanctioning authority (Chapter 4 in this volume).

A second important aspect concerns the engagement with the managerial dimension. We refer not only to the fact that managerialism is an increasingly relevant matter of concern in the academic literature – especially in MOS – where it is either augmented or criticized. Yet, it demands that we reflect on the pronounced managerial orientations of most academic organizations. However, here we want to highlight the centrality of management as one among other privileged objects of inquiry in MOS. Hence, adopting a response-able approach implies devoting specific attention to the moral foundation of management and the social consequences of practicing it to the detriment of marginalized others or others in marginalized contexts (i.e., the Global South) (Chapter 6 in this volume). Accordingly, as response-able researchers, we should care for how dimensions like ethics, responsibility, and sustainability are entangled and enacted in the organizational and management contexts and practices we are confronted with (Gherardi and Lassch 2001). Moreover, we should not limit our scrutiny to individual managers, their work, or the material-discursive circumstances where they operate but rather intra-actively engage with all these elements by appreciating their agential power. Moving in this direction means opening a space for alternatives to dominant paradigms, unveiling criticalities and ambivalences, and stimulating collegial reflection on and creative exploration of how management can otherwise be driven by care and sustainability rather than rationality and efficiency. Response-able management practices stress the mutual obligation of people and organizations to listen and respond to each other (Bozalek 2020), take care of existing vulnerabilities and risks, and resist the rhetoric of grand societal challenges by engaging in collaborative actions instead.

The third domain we would like to highlight is public engagement and academic activism carried out by researchers. Public or community engagement (along with scientific research and education, which are the other key functions of a university) refers to the combination of scientific activities, technological activities, and cultural 'transfer' and the operational transformation of knowledge through which universities activate processes of direct interaction with the territories and communities of competence to contribute to their social and cultural growth with the overall goal of generating mutual benefit. Over the years, these activities have become critical in academia to enforce social responsibility and academic accountability toward different 'stakeholders.' From a response-able perspective, dealing with the heterogeneity of multiple actors implies openness toward diverse subjects, views, and the conditions for which these actions and interventions are designed. Instead of following a commodifying logic of knowledge transfer, ethics of engagement suggests a participative logic of co-construction. Furthermore, the logic of exporting 'best practices' and 'best knowledge' to local communities – which emerges "from hierarchical relations that assume 'rescuing' the 'other' or knowing what is best for the 'other'" (Kuokkanen 2010, 69) – can be replaced by a logic of intimate and respectful engagement with the others. Put differently, ethics of engagement averts 'academic colonization,' resists political pressures, and opposes destructive agendas that currently affect us at a time of rapid corporatization of academia.

Within the third domain of ethics of engagement, we can consider the active involvement and militancy of researchers in political and social causes: from the fight against inequalities to advocacy for human, feminist, and civil rights, to the mobilization for environmental sustainability. Compared to public engagement, which is currently legitimized or even requested (for example, by most funding agencies), militancy and activism are not always welcomed and valued in academia insofar as they seem to depart from the still dominant vision of *S*cience as neutral and objective. Militancy and activism, by definition, bring the researcher 'into the midst,' and this condition is largely perceived as antithetical to scientific trustworthiness. On the contrary, we deem that this activity outside the 'ivory tower' is attuned to ethics of engagement (Bozalek and Zembylas 2023). Participation in social movements and activist groups embodies different care practices that serve specific causes by listening, responding, co-shaping, and mutually transforming each other in an ecological, distributed relationality. In academic activism, agentive capacities are therefore enabled and reinforced through embodied encounters that accommodate feelings of anger, frustration, and discomfort and mobilize affection and solidarity constitutive of positive and joyful energy (Massumi 2015) (Chapter 5 in this volume).

The chapters contained in this book present various forms of response-able academic practices and ethics of engagement, which we briefly present in the following.

The Structure of the Book

The cartographic reading of the concept of response-ability has allowed us to go through its theoretical foundations and development by highlighting the porous boundaries between disciplines and discourses that have contributed to enriching its meaning. The contribution of feminist posthumanist scholars was and still is key to the onto-epistemological articulation of response-ability in MOS and beyond. The authors of the chapters following this introduction acknowledge this legacy and honor it by generously sharing their embodied academic experiences of being and doing together with others. They offer examples of response-able academic practices and ethics of engagement.

In Chapter 2, Emmanouela Mandalaki draws on Joan Tronto's concepts of responsibility and, in considering Donna Haraway's and Karen Barad's elaborations of the notion of response-ability, she problematizes the traditional approaches to knowledge-making practices in organization studies. Drawing inspiration from feminist scholars, she reflects on personal experiences of reviewing and editing beyond authoring. She thus seeks to conceptualize an ethics of un/knowing, whereby authors, research participants, editors, and reviewers are not framed as separate entities but rather as entangled subjectivities moving through social wor(l)ds.

In Chapter 3, Poole, Contu, and Scully engage with the fundamental question, "How can we write together, response-ably, across difference within the neoliberal university?" Drawing on Judith Butler's work and others, the authors share personal experiences of addressing that question in practice. They point out how the marketization and privatization of the academy rely on the pernicious notion of 'accountability' rooted in the idea of combining, calculating, and reckoning. For these authors, working together is a way to escape this logic and develop a different emancipatory notion of accountability and collaborative justice research across difference. Resisting 'sameness,' the authors engage responsibly with others and reveal how meeting each other across the gulfs of neoliberal academia can be an act of love.

In Chapter 4, Leni Grünbaum and Alice Wickström explore response-ability in research fieldwork. They focus on the affective intensities that emerged during a research process where differences in ideas, rhythms, priorities, and abilities led to uncertainty and vulnerability, necessitating an ongoing negotiation of response-ability. The authors illustrate how response-ability in fieldwork may nurture reciprocal relations that arise from tensions instead of privileging consensus and/or unity. Finally, they argue that response-able research can support organizational processes and practices that enhance individual and collective capacities to act, while counter-acting forms of affective contagion that work in disciplinary and diminishing ways.

In Chapter 5, Pellegrinelli and Parolin contribute to the debate about response-ability in MOS by focusing on the relationships between queerness and responsiveness. The authors conceptualize response-ability as a form of *becoming with* that arises between them as researchers and an activist and queer community. Pellegrinelli and Parolin show how the material and affective forces enabled by a theatrical performance enacted an affective connection between the participants (themselves included) and, in doing so, enabled mutual affirmation and care. Inspired by Donna Haraway and Vinciane Despret, the authors assert that one way to increase one's ability to enter a relational mode with multiple others consists of affectively projecting kindness and then enacting affirmative ethics that enables people to express themselves, flourish, and co-become.

In Chapter 6, Marcelo de Souza Bispo engages with the MOS literature on management. By leveraging posthuman practice theory, he elaborates on the idea of management grounded on an ethics of care and response-ability to contrast the ideology of managerialism. According to de Souza Bispo, offering an alternative to a morality of efficiency inscribed in managerialism is key to a moral theory that acknowledges privileges and vulnerabilities and deals with social challenges from a decolonial perspective.

Overall, this book offers vivid examples of feminist posthumanist inquiry into response-ability in organization and management and, through a feminist posthumanist cartographic lens, we – the editors – invite readers to embark on a responsive journey and navigate their academic landscapes.

Recommended Reading

Original Text by Donna Haraway

Haraway, Donna. 2003. *The Companion Species Manifesto. Dogs, People, and Significant Otherness.* Chicago: Prickly Paradigm Press.

Key Academic Text

Braidotti, Rosi, and Hlavajova, Maria. 2018. *Posthuman Glossary.* London: Bloomsbury Academic.

Accessible Resource

Bozalek, Vivienne. 2021. "Rendering Each Other Capable with Vivienne Bozalek." https://www.youtube.com/watch?v=6GQgB0H80Iw

References

Alakavuklar, Ozan Nadir, Dickson, Andrew G., and Stablein, Ralph. 2017. "The Alienation of Scholarship in Modern Business Schools: From Marxist Material Relations to the Lacanian Subject". *Academy of Management Learning and Education* 16: 454–468.

Amrouche, Charlotte, Breckenridge, Jhilmil, Brewis, Deborah N., Burdellaro, Olimpia, Breiding Hansen, Malte, Pedersen, Christina, Plotnikof, Mie, and Pullen, Alison. 2018. "Powerful Writing". *Ephemera: Theory & Politics in Organization* 18(4): 881–900.

Antoni, Anne, and Beer, Haley. 2023. "Ethical Sensibilities for Practicing Care in Management and Organization Research". *Journal of Business Ethics* 190: 279–294. https://doi.org/10.1007/s10551-023-05419-8

Barad, Karen. 2019. "After the End of the World: Entangled Nuclear Colonialisms, Matters of Force, and the Material Force of Justice". *Theory & Event* 22(3): 524–550.

Barad, Karen. 2012. "What Is the Measure of Nothingness? Infinity, Virtuality, Justice/ Was ist das MaJJ des Nichts? Unendlichkeit, Virtualitiit, Gerechtigkeit". *100 Notes – 100 Thoughts* 99. dOCUMENTA (13).

Barad, Karen. 2010. "Quantum Entanglements and Hauntological Relations of Inheritance". *Derrida Today* 3(2): 240–268.

Barad, Karen. 2007. *Meeting the Universe Halfway: Quantum Physics and the Entanglement of Matter and Meaning*. Durham and London: Duke University Press.

Boncori, Ilaria. 2022. *Researching and Writing Differently*. Cambridge: Polity Press.

Bozalek, Vivienne. 2020. "Rendering Each Other Capable". In *Navigating the Post-qualitative, New Materialist and Critical Posthumanist Terrain Across Disciplines: An Introductory Guide*, edited by Karin Murris, 135–149. New York: Routledge.

Bozalek, Vivienne, and Fullagar, Simone. 2022. "Agential Cut". In *A Glossary for Doing Postqualitative, New Materialist and Critical Posthumanist Research Across Disciplines*, edited by Karin Murris, 30–31. London, New York: Routledge.

Bozalek, Vivienne, and Zembylas, Michalinos. 2023. *Responsibility, Privileged Irresponsibility and Response-Ability. Higher Education, Coloniality and Ecological Damage*. Cham: Palgrave Macmillan.

Bozalek, Vivienne, and Zembylas, Michalinos. 2017. "Towards a Response-able Pedagogy across Higher Education Institutions in Post-Apartheid South Africa: An Ethico-Political Analysis". *Education as Change* 21(2): 62–85.

Bozalek, Vivienne, Zembylas, Michalinos, and Shefer, Tamara. 2019. "Response-able (peer) reviewing matters in higher education: A manifesto". In *Posthumanism and Higher Education: Reimagining Pedagogy, Practice and Research*, edited by Taylor & A. Bayley, 349–358. Cham: Palgrave Macmillan.

Braidotti, Rosi. 2019. *Posthuman Knowledge*. Cambridge: Polity Press.

Bruzzone, Silvia. 2021. "A Posthumanist Research Agenda on Sustainable and Responsible Management Education after the Pandemic". *Journal of Global Responsibility*, 13(1): 56–71.

Cano Abadía, Mónica. 2021. "Towards a Feminist and Affective Pedagogy of Vulnerability". *Matter: Journal of New Materialist Research*, 2(2): 102–129.

Carreri, Anna. 2022. "Gender Identity (Dis)order in Dual Precarious Worker Couples: The 'Family Speaking Drawers' Installation". *Ephemera. Theory & Politics in Organization* 22(1): 189–213.

Carstens, Delphi. 2020. "An Ethics of Immanence. Posthumanism and the Politics of Care". In *Posthuman and Political Care Ethics for Reconfiguring Higher Education*

Pedagogies, edited by Vivienne Bozalek and Michalinos Zembylas, 79–90. London: Routledge.

Contu, Alessia. 2020. "Answering the Crisis with Intellectual Activism: Making a Difference as Business Schools Scholars". *Human Relations*, 73(5): 737–757.

Cozza, Michela, and Gherardi, Silvia. 2023. *The Posthumanist Epistemology of Practice Theory*. Cham: Palgrave Macmillan.

Deleuze, Gilles, and Guattari, Félix. 1994. *What Is Philosophy?* Translated by Hugh Tomlinson and Graham Burchell. New York, Chichester, West Sussex: Columbia University Press.

Despret, Vinciane. 2020. "Traits". *Environmental Humanities* 12(1): 186–189.

Despret, Vinciane. 2013. "Responding Bodies and Partial Affinities in Human-Animal Worlds". *Theory, Culture & Society* 30(7/8): 51–76.

Despret, Vinciane. 2008. "The Becomings of Subjectivity in Animal Worlds". *Subjectivity* 23: 123–139.

Despret, Vinciane. 2004. "The Body We Care for: Figures of Anthropo-Zoo-Genesis". *Body & Society* 10(2–3): 11–134.

Despret, Vinciane, and Meuret, Michel. 2016. "Cosmoecological Sheep and the Arts of Living on a Damaged Planet". *Environmental Humanities* 8(1): 24–36.

Gherardi, Silvia. 2019. "Theorizing Affective Ethnography for Organization Studies". *Organization* 26(6): 741–760.

Gherardi, Silvia and Cozza, Michela. 2022. "Atmospheric Attunement in the Becoming of a Happy Object". In *Doing Process Research in Organizations, Noticing Differently*, edited by Barbara Simpson and Line Revsbæk, 16–38. Oxford: Oxford University Press.

Gherardi, Silvia, and Laasch. 2022. "Responsible Management-as-Practice: Mobilizing a Posthumanist Approach". *Journal of Business Ethics* 181: 269–281.

Gherardi, Silvia, and Rodeschini, Giulia. 2016. "Caring as a Collective Knowledgeable Doing: About Concern and Being Concerned". *Management Learning* 47(3): 266–284.

Haraway, Donna. 2016. *Staying with the Trouble. Making Kin in the Chthulucene*. Durham and London: Duke University Press.

Haraway, Donna. 2008. *When Species Meet*. Minneapolis: University of Minnesota Press.

Haraway, Donna. 1988. "Situated Knowledges: The Science Question in Feminism and the Privilege of Partial Perspective". *Feminist Studies* 14(3): 575–599.

Higgins, Marc. 2021. "Response-Ability Revisited: Towards Re(con)figuring Scientific Literacy". In *Unsettling Responsibility in Science Education. Indigenous Science, Deconstruction, and the Multicultural Science Education Debate*, edited by Marc Higgins, 271–316. Cham: Palgrave Macmillan.

Kaasila-Pakanen, Anna-Liisa, Gao, Grace, Jääskeläinen, Pauliina, Mandalaki, Emmanouela, Einola, Katja, Johansson, Janet, Zang, Ling E., and Pullen, Alison. 2023. "Writing Touch. Writing (Epistemic) Vulnerability". *Gender, Work and Organization* 31(1): 264–283.

Kaasila-Pakanen, Anna-Liisa, and Emmanouela Mandalaki. 2023. "Hysterically Y-ours: Reclaiming Academic Writing as a Hysterical Practice". *Organization* https://doi.org/10.1177/13505084231198436

Kuokkanen, Rauna. 2010. "The Responsibility of the Academy. A Call for Doing Homework". *Journal of Curriculum Theorizing* 26(3): 61–74.

Law, John. 2004. *After Method. Mess in Social Science Research*. London, New York: Routledge.

Lenz Taguchi, Hillevi. 2013. "Images of Thinking in Feminist Materialisms: Ontological Divergences and the Production of Researcher Subjectivities". *International Journal of Qualitative Studies in Education* 26(6): 706–716.

Manning, Erin. 2016. *The Minor Gesture*. Durham, London: Duke University Press.

Massumi, Brian. 2015. *The Politics of Affect*. Cambridge: Polity Press.

Mazzei, Lisa A. 2014. "Beyond an Easy Sense: A Diffractive Analysis". *Qualitative Inquiry* 20(6), 742–746.

Pullen, Alison, and Rhodes, Carl (eds). 2015. *The Routledge Companion to Ethics, Politics and Organizations*. London: Taylor & Francis.

Putnam, Linda L., Fairhurst, Gail T., and Banghart, Scott. 2016. "Contradictions, Dialectics, and Paradoxes in Organizations: A Constitutive Approach". *The Academy of Management Annals* 10(1): 65–171.

Rogowska-Stangret, Monika. 2020. "Care as a Methodology. Reading Natalie Jeremijenko and Vinciane Despret Diffractively". In *Posthuman and Political Care Ethics for Reconfiguring Higher Education Pedagogies*, edited by Vivienne Bozalek and Michalinos Zembylas, 13–26. London: Routledge.

Savransky, Martin, and Stengers, Isabelle. 2018. "Relearning the Art of Paying Attention: A Conversation". *SubStance* 47(1): 130–145.

Simpson, Barbara, and Revsbæk, Line. 2022. *Doing Process Research in Organizations*. Oxford: Oxford University Press.

Stengers, Isabelle, Massumi, Brian, and Manning, Erin. 2009. "History through the Middle: Between Macro and Mesopolitics. Interview with Isabelle Stengers. 25 November 2008". *INFLeXions* 3. https://www.inflexions.org/n3_stengershtml.html

St. Pierre, Elizabeth. 2013. "The Posts Continue: Becoming". *International Journal of Qualitative Studies in Education* 26(6): 646–657.

Tronto, Joan. 2020. "Afterword". In: *Posthuman and Political Care Ethics for Reconfiguring Higher Education Pedagogies*, edited by Vivienne Bozalek, Michalinos Zembylas, and Joan Tronto, 153–160. New York: Routledge.

Tronto, Joan. 2015. *Who Cares? How to Reshape a Democratic Politics*. New York: Cornell University Press.

Tronto, Joan. 2012. "Partiality Based on Relational Responsibilities: Another Approach to Global Ethics". *Ethics and Social Welfare* 6(3): 303–316.

Tronto, Joan 1993. *Moral Boundaries. A Political Argument for an Ethic of Care*. New York: Routledge.

Tsing Lowenhaupt, Anna 2015. *The Mushroom at the End of the World. On the Possibility of Life in Capitalist Ruins*. Princeton and Oxford: Princeton University Press.

Van Dooren, Thom, Kirksey, Eben, and Münster, Ursula. 2016. "Multispecies Studies. Cultivating Arts of Attentiveness". *Environmental Humanities* 8(1): 1–23.

Zembylas, Michalinos. 2005. "A Pedagogy of Unknowing: Witnessing Unknowability in Teaching and Learning". *Studies in Philosophy and Education* 24(2): 139–160.

2 Knowledge Creation as Becoming Together in Writing, Reviewing and Editing

Emmanouela Mandalaki

A Few Months Before This Writing Started…

Da: Michela Cozza
Inviato: sabato 6 maggio 2023 13:51
A: Emmanouela MANDALAKI; Barbara Poggio
Cc: Anna Carreri
Oggetto: Re: Response-ability book - group meeting

Dear Emmanouela,
Your response is one among many gifts that this working and thinking together will give us!

Your thoughts are precious and help to appreciate your contribution even more.

Looking forward to reading your manuscript!
Thanks
Michela

From: Emmanouela MANDALAKI
Sent: Σάββατο, 6 Μαΐου 2023 6:28 μμ
To: Anna Carreri; Michela Cozza; Barbara Poggio
Subject: Response-ability book - group meeting

Dear Michela, Anna and Barbara,
Thank you very much for your valuable thoughts and the precious exchange.

My response was only possible thanks to your generous responses, Michela, which were also offered as gifts to me – maybe we are already practicing our response-ability towards one another and knowledge creation rather than just taking about it😊

I look forward to delving into this writing and anxious to see where it will take me now.

Thanks again,
Wishing you a lovely weekend ahead,
Emmanouela

DOI: 10.4324/9781003452485-2

How else could I start writing this chapter on conceptualizing processes of writing, reviewing and editing, as relational practices of *response-ably becoming together,* if not by recognizing the generous responsive and response-able process that I, as an author, had the privilege to share with Anna, Barbara and Michela – editors of this edited volume – while *becoming with* this writing. Reading our email exchanges often these past months brings me in continuous imaginary conversations with all three of them as well as with the theorists that inspire the conceptualization of this chapter. There are so many fleshy dialogical texts animating my thought, before this text is actually written. Hopefully, the excerpts of the email exchanges above offer an organic and relational ground for broader reflexive conversations around the ethics and politics, thereafter ethico-politics, of knowledge creation.

The next sections interweave embodied narratives on personal experiences of writing, reviewing and editing, with feminist perspectives on relational ethics to advance an understanding of knowledge creation centered around shared responsibility and *response-ability* between human and nonhuman ethical subjects (Tronto 1993; Barad 2010) – authors, research participants, reviewers, editors, texts, material and immaterial elements. I develop a feminist argument which seeks to destabilize and unsettle normative paradigms motivating the creation, development, advancement and dissemination of academic knowledge, arguing rather for the need to drive an epistemological shift toward openness and plurality of perspectives rather than closure, absolute truths, ontological and epistemological fixity, in how we stand vis-à-vis the knowledge we create.

Finding Voice in/through the Guts…

When the invite to write this chapter came in, I was experiencing a particularly heavy agenda with multiple writing commitments to come. I *thought* about whether I *should* say 'No' to this honoring invitation to save myself from one more deadline. Saying 'No' is probably what I *should* have done, all things considered, but such *should* was not necessarily in line with my desire. *Should* is often motivated by normative assumptions resulting from rational thinking processes which tend to distance us ethically from one another. And unfortunately, what usually happens in the overworking culture of neoliberal academia is that, especially as women writers, we might often need to let down collaborations and exciting writing projects that matter, just to attend to increasing administrative tasks and externally set objectives that *should* be implemented in the pursuit of competition and excellence (Mandalaki forthcoming). Such response would not resonate with my work ethic as a feminist author who yearns to actively participate in response-able academic conversations with the potential to reframe the ethico-politics of knowledge creation. Writing this chapter would also mean saying 'No' to something else – one cannot do everything after all. Luckily, there were quite a few *'should'* academic tasks to deprioritize.

Laying in my bed on that same evening and closing my eyes put my mind in some kind of 'pause', giving space to this gut feeling. Something whispered 'do it', write this chapter. It was then clear that I *should* do it. It is these whispers that start from some bodily regions, as Hélène Cixous (1991) reminds us, bringing us to our topics and writing, and then we know/feel[1] that this writing *should* be attended to. This 'should' denotes, in my experience, a different ethical orientation, fueled by relational bodies in conversation. Such intra-corporeal knowing, but also *unknowing*, as discussed next, might lead us to engage with each other, with academic writing and knowledge development more broadly, as an act of care, responsiveness and response-ability toward ourselves and others (Bozalek 2020, 135–149), *with* others.

Given that this is a single-authored article, one might ask, whom are you conversing with in writing alone? This might be a valid question, which in the very early years of my academic career was quite present in me. My (short) experience as a writer of feminist, often autoethnographic texts, has taught me though, that writing, even when starting from an autoethnographic position, remains a relational process (Cixous 1993) submitted to the poetics of synesthetic experience between different others (Perezts 2022), carrying a strong ethico-political bearing for the knowledge we create (Kaasila-Pakanen et al. 2023). This destabilizes the authorial "I" (Stanley 1992; Mandalaki 2021), bringing it into conversation with the human and nonhuman others involved in research, including the body of the text, as active interlocutors in this process (Huopalainen 2020; Henriksen et al. 2022). This is certainly not how I was educated as a doctoral student in normative contexts and as an author of papers desk-rejected by editors of top management journals, with often disqualifying and berating comments (especially in relation to my PhD work, with much of which I could not feel aligned onto-epistemologically – which might explain why some of it remains unpublished). This education had offered a view of academia and publishing as a process of 'playing the game' if we wanted to 'be published' (indeed, this would be more of a passive than an active way of embodying academic work). A game usually played behind closed doors and blind review processes sustained by 'the gatekeepers' of academic knowledge 'production' – processes that we need to abide by, as authors (and namely early career, female authors), if we want our papers to see the 'light of the day'.

- *'Do what reviewers ask for'*, some people were saying.
- *'You need to please the editor/s'* had become a standard motto in some of the research and methodology seminars, repeated by more experienced colleagues, academic mentors and often senior PhD candidates.

I was wondering what was happening to this knowledge that was getting massacred in the name of pleasing an editor and two or three anonymous reviewers. But this voice was often muted, as a female PhD student low in the hierarchy. It was hard to fight this back. It required a few years at the start of my career to identify outlets and conversations to add my voice as part of a relational and response-able conversation, like the one we nurtured with the editors of this book. Without any intent to idealize this, considering also the hard work that caring *for/about/with* others might involve, the support of other like-minded feminist authors and colleagues has been instrumental in this process (Mandalaki and Perezts 2022). I am grateful for this!

Re-viewing Embodied Academic Experiences with/ through Response-ability

I remember my first autoethnographic piece's submission to an academic journal. Stress and anxiety about what the reviewers and editors would say were at the highest, especially given the provocative, feminist tone of the text, often denigrated as identity politics or 'dangerous knowledge' (Bell et al. 2020). When the reviews arrived, I took a deep breath and started reading the letter. To my surprise, not only did the reviewers not disqualify the paper but even offered generous ideas for how to develop the argument further, putting forward deeply resonant, sense- and thought-provoking ideas. Reading the editorial letter had brought me into a conversation with the reviewers and the editor – an embodied dance taking place in my innards and transferred to the text, during the revision process, in a creative way which revealed the potentials of this writing. Most importantly, I realized that my breath was not constrained as it often happens when panic, stress or condescending comments take over. Stress and anxiety were still present but in a creative way that brought breathing back to normal, enabling an embodied writing process, which was already deeply relational. Going back to the words of the reviewers and the editors multiple times and reading them in relation to the revised text nurtured resonance. Some passages in these texts caused shivers every time, without fail. It was summertime but the body hair was still delating, trapping a stream of air in proximity to the skin to rebalance the body's temperature. These shivers were a piece of information, taking an active part in this ongoing conversation. They gave the words to respond to the constructive reviews and a hint that the revisions were moving toward the 'right' direction. I am cautious about using the word 'right' here since I don't wish to confer an ethical judgment based upon normative assumptions of *right* or *wrong* actions. On the contrary, this 'right' judgment was more of a sensation, a feeling than a rational thought. It surfaced the potential/s that we hold in our bodies as writers, reviewers and editors to engage into meaningful conversations when we open ourselves to feel, sense, receive, affect and be affected by one another.

Later, in another experience of submitting for review an autoethnographic text, close to my heart, the reviews were conflicting. Both reviewers could see the broad relevance of the argument, pointing toward important directions for consideration theoretically and methodologically, including a more 'rigorous analysis' of the 'data'. It took time to digest these reviews before starting the revisions, probably also because the text was quite personal and some of the comments 'hurt'. I was deeply challenged and experienced a writer's blockage for a few weeks. Reading the reviews daily for about a month and conversing with the reviewers in my dreams when walking or swimming were necessary for figuring out what they 'wanted me to do'. Much of the literature they recommended opened whole new horizons of conceptualization, meaningfully transforming the argument toward a direction that revealed much of its potential for further development. But, I also knew/felt that the body of the text needed to be respected – this crowded place (Stanley 1992), so easily taken for a lifeless object where different individuals – authors, research and field participants, reviewers, editors – exercise their authority, more often than not with no (or very little) consideration of the affective, embodied subjects involved in research. What would it mean to revise the text in a direction that would make it 'likeable' and 'publishable', if this was not what *it* [the text] wanted?

These are difficult questions to answer and surely clear answers are hard to find. In this particular case, it was not a toolkit guide that offered the answers. I knew/felt, though, that beyond considering very carefully the reviewers' and editors' comments, it was also necessary to ensure that these higher-level conversations would not silence the text's voice and thus the voices of the bodies talked about. During the revision, many of these struggles dressed the opening of the revised (and eventually published) version, making me feeling anxious about how the reviewers would respond. Maybe they would think that I was messing with them or not doing enough justice to their comments. This was certainly not the objective. Admittedly, conversing with the reviewers had been greatly formative and creatively discomforting and had made the text's voice even stronger. 'If only they knew', a voice was resounding in my guts! But it was as if many of these feelings were already evaporating behind a blind review process, probably much like some of the reviewers' reactions and feelings on the text's original and revised versions. The response letter, beyond the revised paper, offered a creative space to argue the revision choices. Being doubtful and questioning these choices as per their ability to do justice to 'everyone' – reviewers, editors, the text, my body, the bodies talked about in the text and the reader – were still present. But, maybe it is too ambitious to think that we can satisfy everyone. And maybe it is just fine if we do not; embracing uncertainty and ambiguity as an organic part of the knowledge creation process (Zembylas 2005). This involves as a process of being open to affect and be affected by others (Gherardi 2019), as well as rendering each other capable of responding by recognizing our special situated needs. Haraway (2016) calls such ethical attitude *response-ability*. Was that it?

Later in my career, I started assuming editorial responsibilities as a guest-editor for special issues for critical journals and co-editor for the Feminist Frontiers section of the journal *Gender, Work and Organization*, in collaboration with my dear colleague Alice Wickström – who is the author of a *response-able* chapter in this volume with Leni Grünbaum. Assuming editorial responsibilities offered a different perspective on the knowledge-creation process and was certainly complementary to the experience of reviewing others' work or writing/revising papers as an author. It was an opportunity to contribute to the advancement of feminist knowledge, creating awareness of the complexity of doing so from the standpoint of an individual who is making the 'final call' on whether a paper will eventually see the 'light of the day'. Such responsibility involved hard decisions and (self)doubt, felt in/through the guts. I realized how dangerous it is to hold such 'authority', especially if used to undermine or abuse those dependent on this. It keeps me continuously thinking and reflecting on how as editors, we can use the editorial means available, in ways that open space for dialogue and collaboration instead of closing off debate with and between authors and reviewers. Obviously, some of the papers under my editorial supervision were not developed enough, in my view, to stand major or minor revisions or peer review. Sometimes, it was even unclear whether an invitation to revisions could be offered after reading the reviewers' comments.

Making these decisions, with feminist sensibilities and inspirations, involved enacting *response-ability*, as openness to be attentive, carefull and available to listen to the unknown other (author, research participants, reviewer, methods, theories, etc.) and to respond to their needs by enacting my potential for care (again without any intent to idealize). As an editor, I initially think of and try to feel the author as the last wish would be to embody the editor's example that made me feel useless at the start of my career – those offering disqualifying reviews with no consideration for the emotional toll that this might have on the writer. Unfortunately, many time or most of the time, it is such authority figures that set the examples that we live by as academics, as we often acritically reshuffle and recycle their pompous wording in review and editorial letters when we take over these roles. Luckily though, there were other examples to consider, those of inspiring feminist colleagues whose review and editorial letters had made a difference to me as an author, recognizing the author as an active interlocutor in this debate and not as a passive subject that would have to 'please' the reviewers and the editor/s. Alison Pullen, Jenny Helin, Kat Riach, as well as Anna Carreri, Barbara Poggio and Michela Cozza, the editors of this volume.

Reflecting on these experiences raises questions for editors: How can we enact our capacity to respond and engage in care-full conversations that respect and attend to the author's ideas and positionality in view of a studied context and intended contributions? How can we engage our physical, intellectual and embodied capacities to contribute to advancing the debate theoretically and methodologically, as a process of enacting feminist care and response-ability toward knowledge development itself? The research participants, reviewers and readers who generously participate in this type of conversation from their different positionalities take a central role too. What is the conversation about and how might we enable a process whereby everyone involved could find space to actively raise their voice and listen to each other attentively and openly? What does the author try to say? How and to whom? What do the reviewer/s understand and respond to this and how do they do so? How might the reader add to this debate if the paper is eventually published? How might we, as editors, support in bringing these different views in conversation to generate space for *different* ideas and feelings to be expressed in feminist language? How may we facilitate the nurturance of a relational environment grounded on attentiveness, listening and active dialogue between us all, as part of a response-able process of knowledge generation? What words to choose in an editorial letter to offer a constructive and caring review that enacts my-our ability to care-fully converse with and respond to the other/s involved in the debate? What do we learn and how might this lead us to reconsider not only the arguments put forward in terms of 'literature contributions' but also the process of knowing and knowledge crafting as relational? As a process based on mutual respect, care, relationality, onto-epistemological unfixity and continuous becoming, recognizing our embodied capacity to exist differently and affectively with/through one another (Gherardi 2019) by conversing and responding to each one's special needs.

These are complex questions to ask oneself, and the answers are hard to identify. Notwithstanding the complexity of dealing with such questioning, I argue that it might still be worth posing such questions, though, as a way of destabilizing taken-for-granted assumptions and power dynamics in academic knowledge creation. Navigating this complexity often involves seeking advice from more experienced colleagues and co-editors; as well as un/learning and becoming with everyone involved in the crafting of new knowledge, considering objects, matters and subjects as made and remade through relational entanglements and not as pre-fixed entities with assigned ontological and epistemological stances (Bozalek 2020, 135–149). In pondering these questions, every time a little differently, as authors, editors or reviewers in conversation, we might see different, new pieces of a 'puzzle' continuously under construction. We might consider ideas, situations, theories, methods, research participants, arguments, positionalities, matters and affects in a new light to challenge vested epistemic habits and long-held assumptions that more often than not see knowledge as the final 'product' of a standardized lifeless publication process. This might allow us to open our bodies to be affected by and affect others to engage together in processes of collective learning and unlearning, knowing and unknowing, as well as feeling, sensing, relating and reflecting that point toward new directions.

Presenting the above events is neither to offer these examples as ones that *should* be followed nor to disregard other ways of doing, being and becoming as authors, reviewers and editors. These are exposed with the hope of inviting colleagues and the readers of this text in an ongoing and relational conversation with broader relevance around the ethico-politics of reviewing, editing, publishing and disseminating academic papers in organization studies (e.g., see also Bozalek et al. 2019, 349–358; Lindebaum and Jordan 2022), a conversation which does not consider each of us as passive actors with isolated tasks to be performed and coordinated toward the 'production' of a final text. But one that recognizes knowledge development as a relational endeavor *in the making*, whereby authors, reviewers, editors, research participants, readers, texts, methods, matters, the animals that sit on our laps and keyboards while we are writing, and the cups of coffee or tea that warm our fingers, bringing blood to our texts, coexist, interact and intra-act in forming a complex, unfinished web of being and becoming. Knowledge and knowing might then be reframed as uncertain, playful, surprising, affective, attentive, care-full, response-able and responsive processes in the making, creatively destabilizing the human subject, author, reviewer or editor as the owner/s of knowledge, and bringing forward an onto-epistemological shift with ethico-political potential (see Kaasila-Pakanen et al. 2023) in how to stand vis-à-vis the knowledge we create.

Reframing Knowledge Creation as a Response-able Process of Becoming Together

Reflecting on the above experiences invites a reframing of the conditions of academic knowledge creation in ways that consider the multifaceted relational, ethical, political and affective elements shaping this. As emerging from the above narratives, I argue that knowledge creation is rarely a mono-dimensional or fixed process following clear guidelines and processes. It involves dialogue, collective reflection on ideas and ideally an open attitude that can let *different others'* affective bodies and perspectives in (Pullen and Rhodes 2015; Helin 2019; Mandalaki 2023). When we write/revise papers, we affect and are affected by the editors' and reviewers' comments. These make us think, feel and sense, sometimes leading us to immediately release our creative energies in transforming our texts, and others making us feel completely blocked and unsure about what/how to write/think/feel/know. These complex processes more often than not push us to experience conflicting affects transpiring through our in/visible bodies to the text, hopefully giving us the words to respond and continue the debate. When crafting editorial letters, we are affected by the papers we read and the reviewers' comments on these. We often cut and paste reviewers' comments, 'diffracting[2]' others' texts (Barad 2007, 2014; Enang et al. 2023; van Amsterdam et al. 2023, 76–91), offering additional readings to provide authors with some constructive (hopefully!) ideas for developing their argument/s further. As reviewers, we read papers that make us consider, ponder and feel new things, offering reviews intended to participate in an ongoing conversation. Such embodied living processes of reading, listening, dialoguing and responding to each other's thoughts, ideas and reflections constitute inseparable parts of 'our' academic *becoming* and thereafter 'final' arguments, transforming us/them in often unanticipated ways.

There is also much invisible labor going on behind many of these blind writing and reviewing processes. Reflecting on the above experiences also speaks of all the emotional labor involved in this process, not just the intellectual or cognitive. It is also *a labor of care for and with the others and the created knowledge itself*, evolving in the context of ongoing interactions and intra-actions between authors, research participants, reviewers, editors, affects, texts and matters. It is a conversation, whereby different interlocutors ponder together the potentials of academic arguments to participate in larger scholarly, social and political debates. Such an open attitude might resist comparisons and juxtapositions between theories, writing styles, methodological approaches, authors' and research participants' positionalities (as it usually happens), to embrace new perspectives, ambiguity and difference as integral to the knowledge creation process.

Conceiving of knowledge creation this way requires recognizing that we are capable of responsibly enacting toward each other and the knowledge we create, by reframing responsibility not just as an individual matter but as a relational process shared *with* others (Tronto 1993). This involves being attentive to others' different needs and perspectives, as well as rendering each other capable to identify and respond to our different ethical needs – a practice of *response-ability* (Haraway 2016; Bozalek 2020, 135–149). This argument resonates with feminist authors and theorists questioning conceptions of ethics as a matter of individualistic rational thinking, conceptualizing it rather as a relational process evolving in/through relational, embodied and affective interactions (Tronto 1993; Pullen and Rhodes 2015; Fotaki and Harding 2017) and intra-actions with others (Barad 2010; Haraway 2016; Gherardi 2019). Such intra-activity relies on our ability and even obligation to respond to the human and nonhuman entanglements that we inhabit as vulnerable beings (Barad 2010).

As Joan Tronto reminds us, there are different ways of enacting care as an ethical stance – *caring of, for and about* (see Tronto 1993 for a review) – each based on different assumptions about the relation with the other. Moving beyond normative conceptions of ethics as a mind-driven process or one viewing ethics as purely taking care *of* the other, as a passive agent unreflexively seen in need of help and empathy (see Hemmings 2012 for a reflection on lazy empathy), I argue for the need to recognize care as a process shared *with* others. We might adopt an ethical stance that considers the other's positionality, views, needs and perspectives, as well as the risks, playfulness, surprises, experimentation and open potentialities surrounding human and nonhuman intra-actions (Bozalek 2020, 135–149). In this conception, empathy is not (just) about feeling what the other feels but also about making the body available to receive the response of the other (Despret 2013). As Schrader (2010) argues, the ethics grounded on such conception of care and response-ability does not already 'exist' in the social world or in a particular response driven by the researcher's pre-established intentions. It rather emerges in the "enabling of responsiveness within experimental relatings" (Schrader 2010, 277). Such a stance is motivated by a relational ontology, assuming that entities, objects or subjects come into being through their relationships rather than preceding them (Barad 2007). Embodying such an attitude leads us to approach knowledge and knowing as *making with others,* what Donna Haraway (2016) calls *sympoesis*. This destabilizes the ontological fixity normatively and unreflexively assigned to ethical subjects, inviting us to recognize that as bodies and matters entangled in a sociomaterial web, we can hardly ever observe the world from a distance through the dominance of 'sight', as we are instructed in social sciences (Barad 2007). As Mazzei reminds us, "knowing is never done in isolation but always effected by different forces coming together" (Mazzei 2014, 743), whereby we come to know/sense/feel what/how we know/sense/feel as active participants of the world (Barad 2007). We might thus recognize knowledge creation as a relational, unfinished process of collective-knowing, whereby entangled phenomena, bodies, objects, matters, histories and affects interweave into a complex, fluid web of being and becoming (van Amsterdam et al. 2023, 76–91).

Becoming with the above feminist inspirations thus surfaces an ethics of knowing, whereby authors, editors and reviewers are not normatively understood as separate entities with pre-assigned roles, duties and obligations. Nor are they seen as authority figures that should be blindly 'pleased' without considering the embodied, emotional and intellectual cost for the involved subjects and the consequences for the created knowledge. The ethics of knowing proposed here views knowledge development as a co-creation process between actively involved embodied subjects in conversation. Such conversation also evolves in tandem with theories, methodologies, epistemologies, matters, spaces, events, our cups of coffee or tea, other nonhuman and more-than-human companions and the affective intensities navigated *as we collectively move through social wor(l)ds*. In this conception, knowledge dissemination processes do not fall under the (exclusive) jurisdiction of all-powerful editors and *anonymous* reviewers (Bozalek et al. 2019, 349–358) or are considered the ultimate ownership of authors and publishing houses. They *become* processes 'in the making', in the context of ever-evolving, unfinished and affective encounters between bodies and materialities able to affect and be affected by each other. Such a conception involves recognizing our existences, as editors, reviewers and authors, as inter-dependent, intra-acting and interrelated, as *more than one* body (Gherardi 2019), creatively destabilizing underlying power dynamics. This might make us aware of the epistemic responsibilities we share *for and with* each other, and with the surrounding world – how we research/write, whom we cite or not and what we make visible or invisible through our arguments.

Embracing uncertainty and the endless potentialities of such an ongoing process might lead us to embody epistemic humility and vulnerability in how we involve ourselves (Gilson 2011) in knowledge-making. Acknowledging vulnerability as an epistemic condition (Gilson 2011; see also Kaasila-Pakanen et al. 2023) unsettles the idea(l) of epistemic invulnerability as well as the epistemological closure emerging from this. It allows us to ask questions and consider potentialities not accounted for before; to read, feel, relate and reflect more; and to open up to listen to the perspective of the other, to recognize our capacity to become response-able toward one another in this complex web of intra-active becoming. We might consider subjects' and objects' different positionalities (including research participants'), making space for *different, marginalized* bodies (usually bodies not abiding by heteronormative standards) to be part of academic debates. We may then recognize the impossibility of even knowing others fully, coming to terms not only with what we might know but also with the potentialities of *unknowing* – being receptive and attentive to all that we do not know and might never fully own as knowledge (see Kaasila-Pakanen et al. 2023). Such an epistemic attitude opposes structural marginalizing patterns that construct epistemically disadvantaged identities by subjecting them to processes of epistemic oppression (Dotson 2014; Kaasila-Pakanen and Mandalaki 2023). It proposes rather an epistemological shift with ethico-political bearing, which embraces openness to the perspective/s of the other. In the proposed conceptualization, such a shift does not just involve being self-reflexive about one's positionality as a researcher. It rather considers how a distanced self-reflexive stance might often risk recreating flawed assumptions about the other's actual needs and position, which might have implications for the emergent knowledge and the voices that this knowledge makes visible (and how). The conception put forward here recognizes the importance of multivocal dialogues and affective exchanges grounded on active sharing, listening, feelings, embodied affects, emotions, knowledges, attentiveness as well as empathy, care and a practice of accountability which respect the different parties' ethical needs. This invites reflexivity as a relational process in the making with the other (Mandalaki 2023) – the editor, the author, the theorist, the studied other, the reader but also the methodologies, onto-epistemologies, matters and texts that inspire our processes (Doucet 2007).

Recognizing everyone involved in the knowledge creation as an active agent able to affect and be affected by others resists clear boundaries between ontologies, epistemologies, ethics and politics. It might lead us rather to embrace knowledge creation as a politico-ethico-onto-epistemological endeavor (Bozalek 2020, 135–149; Kaasila-Pakanen et al. 2023). *Becoming with knowledge,* this way, yearns for slowness; it is embedded in temporally unfixed, ever-evolving processes of embodied exchanges and the ethico-political bearing that such intra-activity of/in/through knowing entails. This stresses the temporal aspect of knowledge development which is not limited to the very processes of writing, reviewing or editing but rather considers the spatio-temporally varying phases of feeling, reflecting, dialoguing, writing, rewriting, reviewing and editing involved in this making (as conveyed in/through the above email exchanges). This opposes clear separations between being, becoming and knowing across times and spaces, opening us up to the potentialities of transforming each other through our complex relationships in/through the knowledge we create. It is about enacting our potential of/for knowing, unknowing, learning and unlearning *differently* in connection with vulnerable others; hence, about experiencing and approaching knowledge and learning through a new light in/through/with others, which might lead us to reconsider long-held views and perspectives.

Final Reflections

The above invites us, academics, to consider more empathetic, response-able and response-generative editing and reviewing practices that challenge the idea of the all-knowledgeable, autonomous and unshakable authority of reviewers and editors that 'should be pleased' no matter what. We might resist claims of closure, certainty and absolute truths which we are so comfortably instructed to embody as academic writers, reviewers, and editors of organization studies. We might rather open up to experience creative discomfort and questioning as well as enlist the courage to turn our critical gaze toward ourselves, to question how we might often unconsciously reproduce hierarchies and patterns of marginalization in the knowledge we create and diffuse. It might make a creative difference to conceive of ourselves as active interlocutors of ongoing academic debates and as ontologically unfixed academic subjectivities co-becoming in the making with other authors, research participants, editors, reviews, ideas, theories, matters, methodologies and epistemologies. Such a conception of ethics in knowledge creation also destabilizes individualistic narratives in relation to the ownership of academic texts (Cixous 1993). It leads us to understand ourselves as intra-acting and intra-active facilitators in the making of academic knowledge – maybe as living organisms in the growing body of knowledge and ideas yet to *be-come*.

Such a proposition wishes that all different parties involved in academic knowledge creation are willing to participate in open and ongoing academic debates (which is not always the case), since democratic dialogue requires active and equitable participation by all parties involved. Further, while this writing has not focused much on the role of the readers/audience per se (even though editors and reviewers are among the first readers of academic papers), or the researched populations involved in academic investigations, it recognizes their meaningful contributions in co-shaping academic knowledge, inviting future researchers to consider more fully such entanglements in this ongoing debate. Moreover, hopefully, this text can generate a debate about the usefulness of the blind review process. Does blind review help or inhibit relational editing/reviewing/authoring practices? Does it recognize shared responsibility, response-ability and accountability as the cornerstone of academic knowledge production (see Bozalek et al. 2019, 349–358 for a related discussion)? These are questions that have not been dealt with in this chapter. I would, though, like to take this opportunity to invite the academic community to a reflexive debate around these issues – maybe an attempt to seriously integrate feminist and response-able ways of knowing to reconfigure the bases upon which academic knowledge in organization studies is developed (see Fotaki and Pullen 2023).

I will 'close' this text with some resonant reflections from non-academic texts, which usually offer inspiration when the politics of academic knowledge creation create despair. Novelists and thinkers have reflected on the limitations of knowledge and knowing, probably (well!) before us, discussing how we tend to fall into false illusions of validity and closure, as we strive to navigate the queer gamble of our uncertain existences.

As Iris Murdoch (2001, 477) beautifully puts it, in her novel *The Sea, the Sea*:

> loose ends can never be properly tied, one is always producing new ones. Time, like the sea, unties all knots. Judgements on people are never final, they emerge from summings up which at once suggest the need of a reconsideration. Human arrangements are nothing but loose ends and hazy reckoning.

But here is where we do have a choice, Maria Popova continues, drawing on Murdoch's inspiration: "In accepting a hazy and uncertain reality beyond our control, we can also refuse to resign ourselves to being victims of it" (Popova 2023). Such attitude can be seen as the highest measure of 'unselfing' (i.e., an occasion experienced in interactions with nature and in contemplations of art, Murdoch 2001), recognizing that life is probably more interesting as a process of continuous presence than as an acted drama (whereby we take ontologically fixed positions as victims or perpetrators), more as a shoreline than as a stage. For, it is often at the living shore that we experience (from our different positionalities) the endless voyages of time and the rhythms of the sea … in which there is no finality, ultimate and fixed reality.

… only shoreless seeds and stardust …
(Popova 2023, see also Carson 2003)

Recommended Reading

Original Text by Donna Haraway

Haraway, Donna. 2013. "A cyborg manifesto: Science, technology, and socialist-feminism in the late twentieth century." In *The Transgender Studies Reader*, edited by Susan Stryker and Stephen Whittle, 103–118. New York, London: Routledge.

Key Academic Text

Shefer, Tamara, Vivienne Bozalek, and Nike Romano. 2023. *Hydrofeminist Thinking with Oceans: Political and Scholarly Possibilities*. Abingdon: Taylor & Francis.

Accessible Resource

Barad, Karen. 2016. *Troubling Time/s, Undoing the Future*. Ted talk accessible at https://www.youtube.com/watch?v=dBnOJioYNHU[3]

Notes

1 The use of knew/felt and other similar mentions, where words are separated by a slash, denote some of the ever-present coexisting tensions between our rational and most embodied parts, revealing research as a multifaceted phenomenological endeavor in connection with the surrounding world and materialities, also hinting towards, I believe, a 'lack' of a(n) (academic) language for articulating the unavoidable nonseparateness between these processes.

2 Barad (2007, 30) propose diffraction as an alternative to reflection and reflexivity, as a process that "does not fix what is object and what is subject in advance", as "reading insights through one another in ways that help illuminate differences as they emerge: how different differences get made, what gets excluded, and how these exclusions matter" (see also Bozalek 2020).

3 This talk was given on June 2, 2016 at The School of Culture and Society, Aarhus University, Denmark in the *Futures Lecture Series*.

References

Barad, Karen. 2014. "Diffracting diffraction: Cutting together-apart." *Parallax*, 20(3): 168–187.

Barad, Karen. 2010. "Quantum entanglements and hauntological relations of inheritance. Dis/continuities, spacetime enfoldings, and justice-to-come." *Derrida Today*, 3(2):240–268.

Barad, Karen. 2007. *Meeting the Universe Halfway: Quantum Physics and the Entanglement of Matter and Meaning*. London: Duke University Press.

Bell, Emma, Susan Meriläinen, Scott Taylor, and Janne Tienari. 2020. "Dangerous knowledge: The political, personal, and epistemological promise of feminist research in management and organization studies." *International Journal of Management Reviews*, 22(2):177–192.

Bozalek, Vivienne, Michalinos Zembylas, and Tamara Shefer. 2019. "Response-able (peer) reviewing matters in higher education: A manifesto." In *Posthumanism and Higher Education: Reimagining Pedagogy, Practice and Research*, edited by Carol Tylor and Annouchka Bayley, 349–358. Cham: Palgrave Macmillan.

Bozalek, Vivienne. 2020. "Rendering each other capable: Doing response-able research responsibly." In *Navigating the Postqualitative, New Materialist and Critical Posthumanist Terrain across Disciplines*, 135–149. London: Routledge.

Carson, Rachel. 2003. *The Sea Around Us*. USA: Oxford University Press.

Cixous, Hélène. 1993. *Three Steps on the Ladder of Writing*. New York: Columbia University Press.

Cixous, Hélène. 1991. *Coming to Writing and Other Essays*. New York: Harvard University Press.

Despret, Vinciane. 2013. "Responding bodies and partial affinities in human–animal worlds." *Theory, Culture & Society*, 30(7/8):51–76. https://doi.org/10.1177/0263276413496852.

Dotson, Kristie. 2014. "Conceptualizing epistemic oppression." *Social Epistemology*, 28(2):115–138. https://doi.org/10.1080/02691728.2013.782585

Doucet, Andrea. 2007. "From her side of the Gossamer Wall(s): Reflexivity and relational knowing." *Qualitative Sociology*, 31(1):73–87.

Enang, Etieno, Harry Sminia, Silvia Gherardi, and Ying Zhang. 2023. "Unpacking researchers' embodied sensemaking: A diffractive reading-writing of Mann Gulch disaster." *Scandinavian Journal of Management*, 39(4):101–299.

Fotaki, Marianna and Alison Pullen. 2023. "Feminist theories and activist practices in organization studies." *Organization Studies*, 01708406231209861.

Fotaki, Marianna and Nancy Harding. 2017. *Gender and the Organization: Women at Work in the 21st Century*. Abingdon: Routledge.

Gherardi, Silvia. 2019. "Theorizing affective ethnography for organization studies." *Organization*, 26(6):741–760.

Gilson, Erinn. 2011. "Vulnerability, ignorance, and oppression." *Hypatia*, 26(2):308–332.

Haraway Donna, Jeanne. 2016. *Staying with the Trouble: Making Kin in the Chthulucene*. Durham: Duke University Press.

Helin, Jenny. 2019. "Dialogical writing: Co-inquiring between the written and the spoken word." *Culture and Organization*, 25(1):1–15.

Hemmings, Clare. 2012. "Affective solidarity: Feminist reflexivity and political transformation." *Feminist Theory*, 13(2):147–161.

Henriksen, Line, Katrine M. Kjær, Marie Blønd, Marisa Cohn, Baki Cakici, Rachel Douglas-Jones, Pedro Fereira, Viktoriya Feshak, Simy Kaur Gahoonia, and Sunniva Sandbukt. 2022. "Writing bodies and bodies of text: Thinking vulnerability through monsters." *Gender, Work & Organization*, 29(2):561–574.

Huopalainen, Astrid. 2022. "Writing with the bitches." *Organization*, 29(6):959–978.

Kaasila-Pakanen, Anna-Liisa, and Emmanouela Mandalaki. 2023. "*Hysterically y-ours*: Reclaiming academic writing as a hysterical practice." *Organization*, https://doi.org/10.1177/13505084231198

Kaasila-Pakanen, Anna-Liisa, Grace Gao, Pauliina Jääskeläinen, Emmanouela Mandalaki, Katja Einola, Janet Johansson, Ling E. Zang, and Alison Pullen. 2023. "Writing touch. Writing (epistemic) vulnerability." *Gender, Work and Organization*. https://doi.org/10.1111/gwao.13064

Lindebaum, Dirk and Peter Jordan. 2023. "Publishing more than reviewing? Some ethical musings on the sustainability of the peer review process." *Organization*, 30(2):396–406.

Mandalaki, Emmanouela. 2023. "Invi(α)gora ting reflexivity in research: (Un) Learnings from α field." *Organization Studies*, 44(2):314–320.

Mandalaki, Emmanouela and Mar Pérezts. 2023. "Abjection overruled! Time to dismantle sexist cyberbullying in academia." *Organization*, 30(1):168–180.

Mandalaki, Emmanouela. 2021. "Authorize me to write: Going back to writing with our fingers." *Gender, Work & Organization*, 28(3):1008–1022.

Mandalaki, Emmanouela. forthcoming. "Feminist thoughts before annual leave." In *Genderwashing in Leadership: Practices, Policies, and Politics*, edited by Rita Gardiner and Wendy Fox-Kirk, 9–13. Leeds: Emerald Publishing.

Murdoch, Iris. 2001. *The Sea, the Sea*. New York: Penguin.

Pérezts, Mar. 2022. "Unlearning organized numbness through poetic synesthesia: A study in scarlet." *Management Learning*, 53(4):652–674.

Popova, Maria. 2023. "Iris Murdoch on the myth of closure and the beautiful, maddening blind spots of our self-knowledge." *The Marginalian*, September 17th, 2023 https://www.themarginalian.org/2022/06/23/iris-murdoch-the-sea-the-sea/.

Pullen, Alison. 2018. "Writing as labiaplasty." *Organization*, 25(1):123–130.

Pullen, Alison and Carl Rhodes. 2015. "Ethics, embodiment and organizations." *Organization*, 22(2):159–165.

Schrader, Astrid. 2010. "Responding to *Pfiesteria piscicida* (the fish killer): Phantomatic ontologies, indeterminacy, and responsibility intoxic microbiology." *Social Studies of Science*, 40(2):275–306.

Stanley, Liz. 1992. *The Auto/Biographical I: The Theory and Practice of Feminist Auto/Biography*. Manchester and New York: Manchester University Press.

Tronto, Joan C. 1993. *Moral Boundaries: A Political Argument for an Ethic of Care*. Routledge.

van Amsterdam, Noortje, Katrine M. Kjær, and Dide van Eck. 2022. "Becoming with Barad: A material-discursive-affective conversation." In *Affect in Organization and Management*, edited by Carolyn Hunter and Nina Kivinen, 76–91. New York: Routledge.

Zembylas, Michalinos. 2005. "A pedagogy of unknowing: Witnessing unknowability in teaching and learning." *Studies in Philosophy and Education*, 24(2):139–160.

3 Collaborative Justice Research across Difference

Jared M. Poole, Alessia Contu, and Maureen A. Scully

Introduction

How do scholars separated by sociopolitical differences—of race, gender, class, etc.—transcend those differences to do justice work? How can this be accomplished response-ably, mutually accentuating one another's agency without reproducing power dynamics that pervade an unjust status quo? Writing and working collaboratively across difference is, for us, fundamentally a matter of knowing others and being known by others. For this reason, we begin our chapter with the notion of *accountability*. This word is etymologically rooted in "count," from the Latin *computere* (*com* meaning "together," and *-putere* meaning "to think"), hence the idea of combining, calculating, and reckoning (Oxford English Dictionary). Accounting, which invokes a flat stock-taking, is a word whose English origins are imbued with "thinking together." Is it even possible to do that *together*? Yet it is in a kind of togetherness—dubious, uncertain, dangerous—that accounting takes place. The act of accounting is always relational. It posits oneself and the other in a relation where there is a demand, an address to give an account of oneself to another (Butler 2005). Desire is also at stake. Desire for recognition—to be heard, to be seen, to be loved?—in that place where this togetherness, as unclear, opaque, and unsettling as it is, is established. Inevitably (yet variably, in different spatial/time coordinates), expectations, norms, values, a certain mode of conduct, get played out in accounting.

In this chapter, we probe varying senses of accountability, at the heart of response-ability, including accountability to ourselves, to one another, to our organizations, and to our communities. At present, accountability in the neoliberal academy is the most obvious and familiar one in our profession, given its hegemonic status. Establishing and providing a measurable record of the self and of life is central to this accountability—how many publications, how many citations, and what is the score on the teaching evaluations? We discuss this version of accountability where life is cut into countable units to be consumed in reproducing the status quo. Then we move on to elaborate, in and through our writing, an emancipatory conception of accountability. Writing

DOI: 10.4324/9781003452485-3

together, working together to unsettle that status quo, and opening spaces for flourishing institutes an accountability that we recognize and thematize in this chapter. In it, the togetherness established, with the terrifying gulf made obvious by the exposure and vulnerability at stake, is faced in the work, in the practices making each of us for each other, and for the world we are prefiguring together. We think with Judith Butler's discussion of responsibility in giving an account of oneself to another by considering it not only an ethical act but also a political one exactly because of the critical tension and the prefiguration of ourselves and the world in our practices. Many other thinkers also join our conversation as we move to consider the significance of time and love for emancipatory accountability in our scholarly work.

Throughout, we as authors figure prominently as our argument developed within and through our collaborative scholarship. Therefore, we begin by briefly outlining who this "we" is. We differ along many dimensions. Some of the most salient, given our context and the nature of our work, pertain to race, national/regional origin, gender, age, career stage, and academic background. We share an institutional context, working in the same department at an urban public university in Boston, Massachusetts. More importantly, we also share a broad commitment to promoting liberty, equality, and solidarity through our work. Cashing out what this means through our work (how do we enact our shared values?) is the central puzzle that guides this chapter.

Accountability in the Neoliberal Academy

Arguably, the challenge of knowing and being known is just what scholarship is about. Certainly, that is the sense given by such stock phrases as "making a theoretical contribution" and "knowing the literature." And there is some truth to that sense. However, it is also the case that the neoliberal academy puts up barriers to genuine mutual reckoning. By "neoliberalism" we refer to the societal ideological trend toward individualism, marketization, privatization, and criminalization, with rallying phrases like "meritocracy" as part of this ideology. The neoliberal system, in our U.S. context, is felt in the defunding of public higher education, where students are transformed into (indebted) consumers, faculty is progressively casualized, disempowered, and subject to increased pressure to conduct scholarship that "pays off" as the impact agenda takes hold of higher education (Smith et al. 2020). Measures of performance based on standardization and quantification have become ubiquitous. In this "tyranny of metrics" (Muller 2018), accountability is given in systems of countable outputs, such as number of publications in high impact factor journals, citations, Altmetric data, h-index, number of grants, number of products, services, "solutions" with and for the business community, and teaching evaluations. For those of us who write in business schools, we become "accountable for our production" in the form of the "valorization of research" that is published in a shrinking list of mainstream journals (Alakavuklar, Dickson, and Stablein 2017, 457). Neoliberal accountability ties our subjectivity (our sense of self and self-worth) to these performance measures, exemplified in and reproduced through the values of individualism and competition which promote narcissism, extractivism, and exploitation of self and others.

Hiring and promotion increasingly rely on performance matrixes based on data that are often spurious, hardly withstanding the rigor of quantitative research. As tenure evaporates, academic careers become increasingly precarious and egoism, instrumentalism, and heightened competition reign (Giroux 2014). University managers caught in the frenzy of such things as university rankings, and national teaching and research evaluation programs support shortsighted strategies and practices which, through goal displacement and other mechanisms, have deleterious effects on the quality of research and teaching (Muller 2018, 77). This system, incidentally, engenders the reproduction of a ballooning administrative/managerial university cadre, ranking organizations, national and international students' procurement agencies, and other accessories to the core function of higher education that keeps inflating university costs. Such costs are borne by students as astronomically high tuition fees and by faculty and staff as stagnating salaries and work intensification. On occasion the "gaming" of this accountability regime rises to the level of official scandal; as was the case in 2022 when Columbia University was delisted from the U.S. News & World Report for providing misleading data; or when in 2021 the Dean of Temple Business School was found guilty of fraud for rigging the numbers to advance in the MBA rankings.

The imprint these expectations leave on the way that scholarship and education go forward has many contours. With Giroux (2014, 61) we note that neoliberal corporate and market-driven forces operate to destroy higher education as a democratic public sphere. And more broadly the logic of profit-making for private accumulation and consumerism advances commodification and disposability of human and nonhuman life in ways that hollow out *all* democratic processes, learning, and values while ushering in authoritarianism and polarization.

As scholars in a public, urban university that was founded in the 1960s in the wake of the Civil Rights Movement and the deepening demands for justice and democracy for all, we feel keenly the significance and responsibility of working for a continuing democratic revolution in the Commonwealth and beyond. This democratic interest is thwarted by the way that historical injustices—surrounding the exploitation of women (Acker 1990), Black and Brown people (Muzanenhamo and Chowdhury 2023), indigenous people (Peredo 2023), nonhuman animals (Tallberg and Hamilton 2022), and the environment (Nyberg, Wright, and Bowden 2023)—that have always been present in management academia due to its involvement in the development of Western capitalism are maintained and reconstituted, as this pernicious form of accountability seeps into the space between us as writers and mediates our relationships with one another. An emancipatory conception of accountability—a way of knowing and being known that generates collaborative activity toward justice, thus embodying response-ability—that is attuned to the material conditions scholars face is therefore necessary.

Toward an Emancipatory Conception of Accountability

The necessity of this emancipatory form of accountability is generated and emerges in the practices of our work where we are thrown into life paths and circumstances and, more or less conscious choices, to work together. In these practices, we face each other in ways that are uncomfortable as our bodies and conduct falter in following the prescribed scripts of the status quo. Remaining exposed and vulnerable, our bodies and our conduct reveal hints of deviation and resistance to the egotistical demands of doing our work instrumentally and compliantly. As Butler (2005, 31–32) puts it, mobilizing Adriana Cavarero's relational politics and ethics, "we are beings who are, of necessity, exposed to one another in our vulnerability and singularity, and (…) our political situation consists in part in learning how best to handle—to honor—this constant and necessary exposure."

Flashes of recognition that we might be each other's comrades in unsettling and transforming the norms of conduct become tentative invitations to be more intentional and proactive in our encounters. Crucially, emancipatory accountability emerges and remains in the relationality of our being-together—exposed and vulnerable in doing our academic work. The relational encounter at work is not resolved in the recognition of an imaginary "we," for example, *qua* "scholars critical of the neoliberal status quo." While critique is important to each of us, this is not a sufficient source of inscription for a collective discourse where we recognize each other. The political significance of the collective "we" certainly remains, however, central in prefiguring a radical democratic deepening and rearticulation. For that reason, it is even more important to inhabit an emancipatory accountability imbued in "an altruistic ethics of relation" as Cavarero calls it (cited in Butler 2005, 34), each facing the other's singularity by remaining in the question: Who are you? In this question one reflexively resists the dissolution of differences and uniqueness in sameness, while recognizing the political power of articulation for collective action and coordination.

Arguably, the significance of emancipatory accountability became clear to us exactly because of our differences—the gulf, fear, and desire in facing each other in our different backgrounds. We, as collaborators and colleagues, remain deeply ignorant of each other's lives and stories narrating who we are. Yet we are thrown into working together, both organizationally and in causes that became shared. Each could, would, and did mobilize discourses of social justice especially around issues of anti-racism, class exploitation, and sexism that enabled recognizability to be established and maintained and work organized. These functioned as our initial encampments for coordinated activities. Our intentionality in doing this work *together* has become firmer as we try to critically engage the status quo.

But how do we do this well? Response-ably? What does this heightened intentionality look like? To address these questions, we share our story and hope that it illuminates something about your own experiences that helps you to bring justice to your part of the world. We structure our reflections around the different aspects of our work that we have had to "face." When we come together intentionally, with the goal of figuring out what it means to be together and do emancipatory work, we need to countenance one another and our differences. Being different people, in different places, and from different places, recognizing and loving one another for who we are as embodied and embedded is a necessary and continuous movement. The work of coalition building across difference is not easy. We find enormous inspiration for how to do this work in "transversal politics," the practices of "rooting" and "shifting" articulated by pacifist, transnational feminists who constituted a tight net of relations among Palestinian and Israeli women (Lamberti 2019; Yuval-Davis 1999). The "rooting" regards the deep sharing and recognition of each other's stories. With and through a deep and meaningful rooting one also practices dialogue for a shifting, learning to see the other viewpoint, "walking in her shoes." This is something impossible that becomes possible with imagination. Imagination allows moves in time and space, to see a different situation and potentially a new self through which one can return to the dialogue at hand, as Cynthia Cockburn (2015) puts it in elaborating her studies of women using these feminist transversal practices in conflict situations in Northern Ireland, Bosnia-Herzegovina, and Cyprus. Such inspiring practices need to be learned—response-abilities that we co-develop and co-construct while we, as Collins (2013) suggests, engage our ideas (our theories, research findings, etc.) in a praxis that serves social, economic, and epistemic justice (Contu 2020).

Facing Our Academic Structures: Organizations and Organizing

Although neoliberalism is powerful and pervasive, we resist the temptation to reify its features or treat them as inevitable (Fisher 2009). Organizations are expressions of ongoing activity, deliberate and accidental. Knowing this, we have decided to intentionally organize within our organization, through our ongoing establishment over the past two years of a quasi-formal group of students and faculty who work toward justice in their research, teaching, and service. We named this collaborative the Equity, Diversity, Justice, and Inclusion Lab. We refer to it with the acronym "EDJI," to signify that we are sometimes seen as "edgy," we aspire to be on the cutting edge, and we are certainly sometimes a bit on edge when the forces preferring the status quo push back on us. In this group, we aim to be allies—or more provocatively in Bettina Love's (2020) term "co-conspirators"—for one another and with others for whom action toward justice is vital. Being a co-conspirator, Love emphasizes, is about taking responsibility for actions; it is more about the verbs and the brave clashes than what the noun "ally" conveys.

Our rationale behind EDJI was perhaps twofold. First, it creates a structure that all of us EDJI members recognize and respond to. For many of us, our living and working conditions are increasingly precarious and under-resourced. Consequently, we respond to incentives to restrict our attention to the narrow aims that the academy readily values. Even when this incentivization motivates us to do justice-oriented research and teaching, it tends to breed isolation and individualism. Our work is assimilated into the system, and neoliberalism hums along unimpeded. The EDJI Lab, as a symbol that occupies our personal planners (or "productivity apps"), a virtual space where we gather, and a brand that can be made to "count" in certain personnel matters aims to crack into this logic and redirect some of its energies to better ends. The lab's branding is itself a second justification for this organizing structure. We thought it useful to gather under a label that we can project to like-minded scholars and practitioners outside our organization to facilitate collaboration.

Facing Our Academic Communities: What's the Right Thing to Do?

The three of us are tenured or tenure-track faculty, so the communities we face—students, colleagues, and the public—and the way we encounter them reflect our characteristic formal duties. A challenge is to remain reflexive on the relative power we hold compared to many members of these communities. Although neoliberalism comes for us all, it comes for some more quickly and violently than others; indeed, this differential treatment is the foundation of a divide-and-conquer logic that ensures its smooth functioning. Therefore, we attempt to be wary of how we are incentivized to exploit others and we try to use our privileged positions to intervene in these systems countering such exploitation.

Students

Our students are in many ways the most significant "other" we face. They are an "other," who constantly and inexorably shake us from any complacency we might otherwise enjoy in taking our dutiful place in the neoliberal academy. Ultimately, even in the increasingly precarious contracts, inflation, housing costs, and terrible public transport, our conditions are still comfortably middle-class. The neoliberal academy, in Boston, in our public "majority-minority" university, mostly male, middle-class bubble of Whiteness (Muzanenhamo and Chowdhury 2023) is persistently broken by our students who do not fit the image and the norm. Just as the three of us with our bodies (our gender expressions, our complexions, our accents) unsettle the academic norm and with our acts question and resist the norms and conduct that traditional management education imposes on us, so do our students. They address us with a demand to show up for them and to recognize them for who they are so that we can meet them where they are in doing together a meaning-full learning journey to transform both students and us as educators in the process (Freire 1994).

This is not easy, primarily because they are heterogeneous in ways that each of us had not encountered in our prior university life. The neoliberal university catalogs them in institutional statistics and socio-historical orderings. Students are in the majority people of color, many descendants of those forced into slavery from Africa, and many are part of old and new migrant communities to the USA. The majority of our students are the first in their families to go to university. Many work, as well as study, full-time. Some experience hardships that we, as probably most of the readers, have never experienced, such as food insecurity. These categories and orderings weigh on and "make" the students, inviting expectations, forging paths of exclusions and inclusions, opportunities for (and barriers to) agency for them *and* for us. On these "given paths" is where we play out our ethico-political response-ability to locate agency in relationship with our students. We strive to remain accountable to the encounter, who we face, the complexities and unique singularity exposed to each of us as we expose ourselves in the educational encounter.

A few examples illustrate what we find at that encounter: a student asks to meet outside of class to share that the case study on sweatshops and the exploitation of child labor was too close for comfort as they experienced those very circumstances; another discloses that they are homeless and this complicates their ability to be fully present and prepared in class; and another, like so many of them, answers that they are struggling to submit the assignments on time because on top of their full-time studies, they also work full-time and have care responsibilities; yet another struggles with the unpleasantness of a highly coveted, hard-won internship that turns out to be useless in terms of actual learning and upon questioning the broker she is chastised as ungrateful and out of line. In such moments, the pedagogical process, plan, and content must shift. It must move from a "portable" pedagogical model to one that enacts a situated pedagogy that meets the students where they are. The former, in its hegemonic status, can mostly ignore intersecting penalties and opportunities affecting students and reduces differences, for example, of gender, racioethnicity, histories, and class, at best, to topics acknowledged as part of an "inclusive" curriculum. The latter instead is sensitive and attuned to the historical, social, and political vicissitudes at stake for students and educators. In our case, within the specific socio-historical coordinates where we are situated, this means to thematize and counter the systems of inequities that weigh on our students' lives, impeding their learning.

We approach this task in a variety of ways. For example, this situated pedagogical perspective acknowledges and recognizes the richness of students' diversity, by making sure that their bodies, histories, and knowledges are integral to the curriculum; that their experiences and knowledges are central to the learning process; that dialogue, active listening, and perspective-taking are practiced as valued teaching methods. Meeting the students where they are also invites flexibility in learning modalities and assignment structures, including timing and opportunities for meeting us.

Colleagues

Being overtly nonconfrontational is generally sound political advice, and this makes working to change the status quo especially tricky. In this, we are aided by the fact that our university has a progressive history and mission and a still solid union. All of this works to our advantage because it means we can be open with our colleagues about our conception of scholarship and our proposals for improving how our university serves democratic ends. Despite the neoliberal hollowing out of higher education, the dual-governance system remains protected and is still robustly enacted. Cost-cutting shrinks the headcounts; the silver lining is that we all have plenty of service obligations, allowing us to directly shape how the university operates. The three of us, for example, after working for years (with others) to advance diversity and inclusion in hiring and promotion and addressing sexual and racial discrimination, co-signed a motion approved by the College Faculty Assembly to institute a standing committee dedicated to fostering justice, equity, diversity, and inclusion in the College. It is early days to assess the impact of this organizational and institutional change, but it should be noted that this is the first ever of its kind in the college. Another useful vehicle for us is our faculty union which is part of the Massachusetts Teachers Association. Jared at present serves as a union representative on the Executive Committee. Thankfully, many of our colleagues feel the same way, with the majority of them being members—yes, even in the business school (that is New England's pro-labor spirit).

Public

The public is a rather broad "other" and we face it in different ways. As we discuss later, issues of differing time trajectories impinge on our availability to engage meaningfully with the public in ways that do not simply feed the accountability machine of the neoliberal university but are culturally rich and empowering opportunities to deploy our knowledge and skills in deepening the democratic revolution.

For example, both Jared and Maureen have taught an entry-level university class to high school students in local Boston public schools, as an important service to the community. Alessia was a co-organizer of a parent-led group focused on addressing implicit bias, countering systemic racism, and empowering children, teachers, and parents to embrace difference and diversity in the public-school community of her town. She currently serves in the Commission for Diversity and Inclusion of her town. Its goal is to support a welcoming environment by encouraging cooperation, tolerance, and respect among and by all persons who come in contact with the town (visitors, residents, employers, employees, etc.) by advancing, promoting, and advocating for the human and civil rights of all through education, awareness, outreach, and advocacy.

Facing Ourselves: Conclusions about Writing across Difference

Spacetime

What we have hungered for was not a sense of purpose but time. Workload pressures, as public higher education funding and staffing grow leaner, make it harder to find time. Mobilization has always been a matter of time—how to gather people together in a time and place, beyond the demands of work and life, and beyond the gaze of authorities. As Oscar Wilde famously quipped, "The problem with socialism is that it takes up too many evenings." How to find the time? That is some of the practical advice in *Rules for Radicals* (Alinsky 1971) and other toolkits for would-be activists. Here, we offer some reflections on time itself—like light, perhaps it can be both a particle and a wave—as an element in writing collaboratively about and across differences.

Our language sometimes induces us to forget the subtle and impactful ways in which time shapes justice work. The language people typically use to talk about differences revolves around location. Words like "distance," "positionality," and "intersectionality" conjure images of landscapes where each person is differently located relative to others on the canvas. These images of locations shape how we talk about our "standpoint" or "point of view," ocular metaphors that tempt us to think of a snapshot in time or a static image. Responding to this critique, Holvino (2010) offers the concept of "simultaneity" and envisions a hologram instead of a crossroads. Holvino's insight conjures the specter of time. Fluidity or motion becomes the focal dimension of difference (or the mode through which difference is expressed).

How, then, does time relate to the response-able countenancing of difference? Marxist theorists' insights about time are generative for us. Capitalism regards time primarily as an input for commodity production. The commodification of labor into units of time was at the heart of the capitalist system and the creation of the modern factory mentality of clocked-in hours and work production (Landes 1969). This conceptualization of time explains much of what is frustrating, or alienating (Alakavuklar et al. 2017), about academic work—it is dehumanizing in the sense that it fundamentally lacks a human character with respect to time (Debord 1967/2016, 160). This alienation is augmented by the fact that time is just one of many inputs to production. Its real significance becomes ambiguous as it is reduced to its quantitative "exchangeable character" (Debord 1967/2016, 147) yielding a sense of time and memory "that is infinitely plastic, capable of reconfiguring itself at any moment" as the need arises or as other inputs to the production equation change (Fisher 2009, 54). Time is money. Nothing more, nothing less.

So, when we are writing across differences, we are writing across different locations in spacetime. We are writing across different calendars and clocks, biological, personal, social, and professional, that correspond to the material setting (space) in which we must work to survive (and hopefully flourish). These are not calendars we have freely chosen. Only a "false consciousness of time" (Debord 1967/2016, 158) ignores how these calendars are imposed upon us by conditions not of our choosing. Nevertheless, through our work, we make choices and construct a sense of time that we are ultimately accountable for.

What separates us, then, is a breakdown in the meaning of time. Thus, writing across differences, response-ably, is about reorienting ourselves to one another by reconstructing social memory and a shared vision of the future. Piecing together a common history and constructing a shared vision are interrelated tasks. Imagined futures are constructed out of social raw material, and to be compelling must have a plausible connection to the past. There must be some relationship among past, present, and future that all can recognize (and as different ways of knowing emerge, even past, present, and future may not be linearly related but recursively and concurrently flowing). A central activity of accountability, then, is the exchange of narratives, sharing accounts of ourselves and the world around us. Where in spacetime are we? Where are you? How did we get here? Addressing these questions is a core activity in constructing a shared vision of the future ("where are we going?"), such that we mutually equip one another to respond to our circumstances in a way that brings about an aspirational future.

It is worth noting that much about our working conditions discourages this kind of accountability. It requires trust and an investment of time to overcome the distances between us, but these are exactly the things that cost us so dearly in the neoliberal academy. Whom do I trust when social bonds have melted into air? And who has the time?

Values

As we commit time and space to our relationships to create the possibility of writing across differences, we find that one of the principal things we are seeking is alignment in values. Many management scholars are frustrated with the status quo, and our discipline can support a variety of value systems. Consequently, we observe diverse critiques of the prevailing order of things and prescribed alternatives. This diversity is beneficial at least to the extent that it opens more possibilities for improving the world, but it presents a challenge to the individual scholar looking for an intellectual home, community of comrades, or co-conspirators (Love 2020) as a base for doing this work. Among the many raising a critique of mainstream management scholarship, who can I count on to share with me a certain vision of the future? This question is about values. It is not limited to theory or epistemology but takes into consideration how people relate to one another as they go about the work. Recounting cross-race relationships from her youth, bell hooks (1994) describes the simplicity and intimacy of this alignment:

> [W]e shared a similar take on reality. Racial difference meant that we had to struggle to claim the integrity of that bonding. We had no illusions. We knew there would be obstacles, conflict, and pain. In white supremacist capitalist patriarchy […] we knew we would have to pay a price for this friendship, that we would need to possess the courage to stand up for our belief in democracy, in racial justice, in the transformative power of love […] There was no elaborate postmodern political theory shaping our actions. We were simply trying to change the way we went about our everyday lives so that our values and habits of being would reflect our commitment to freedom.
>
> (hooks 1994, 25–26)

What unites people across differences is a kind of accountability or sharing "a similar take on reality." Giving accounts of the world that make sense to one another is not solely, or even primarily, about espousing similar theoretical commitments, but rather embodying compatible values in everyday interactions with others, challenging the taken-for-granted neoliberal order, and enacting a new vision of academia. This web of on-the-ground practices to change stubborn institutions (hooks 1994, 27) is not easy to weave, however. It is underwritten by "struggle and sacrifice" (hooks 1994, 33). Enduring through this struggle is an expression of hope insofar as it begins with the assumption of good faith and solidarity in the other and the expectation of a better future.

Love

What will sustain us during such "struggle and sacrifice?" Neoliberalism motivates by dangling in front of people the prospect of wealth and status, of having it all. Of course, as we have argued, in view of emancipatory notions of accountability, this incentive regime will not do. Rather, what grounds our fight for time and space, in the everyday work of seeking to know and be known, is love.

What's love got to do with it? Meritocracy is all about ranking and sorting and then giving out different rewards accordingly. In this lifetime litany of judgments and evaluations, generating the "hidden injuries of class" (Sennett and Cobb 1972), individuals can be looked down upon as being in the place the meritocracy says they "deserve" (Daniels 1978). The imagined meritocracy was indeed a grim place, from the first satirical use of the word "meritocracy" (Young 1959). This competitive and punitive model of relating to one another makes little room, if any, for mutual struggle and sacrifice with and for the other because it rests on assumptions of individualism. Against this model, response-ability requires recognition of the tragic character of life:

> Life is tragic simply because the earth turns and the sun inexorably rises and sets, and one day, for each of us, the sun will go down for the last, last time. Perhaps the whole root of our trouble, the human trouble, is that we will sacrifice all the beauty of our lives…to deny the fact of death, which is the only fact we have.
>
> (Baldwin 1963/1993, 91)

For Baldwin, the challenge of living is shedding illusions, and the central illusion is that our time to make things right is unlimited. Moreover, the "invidious distinctions" that are the pride of late capitalism prove to be childish fantasies in view of our fundamental equality with respect to death (is it any wonder, then, that the ultra-rich are so preoccupied with transhumanism and other 21st century searches for the Fountain of Youth?). Individualism loses its luster. But facing others is scary because genuine encounters threaten our illusions—that our position is deserved or that neoliberal accountability is the best that we can aspire to. However, love "takes off the masks that we fear we cannot live without and know we cannot live within," allowing relationships of "quest and daring and growth" to take root (Baldwin 1963/1993, 95). Here, Baldwin indicates what is required for academics in the neoliberal academy to do work that is not only interesting but builds toward a better world for future generations.

Love involves risk, but it is a necessary risk if we are to become fully response-able for each other. Loving others is necessarily indeterminate and incomplete because we cannot give a full accounting of possible futures. As a categorical rejection of confining illusions, love is a gamble, but it is guaranteed to be the only way to live with integrity amidst tragedy.

Recommended Reading

Original Text by Karen Barad

Barad, Karen. 2007. *Meeting the Universe Halfway: Quantum Physics and the Entanglement of Matter and Meaning*. Durham, NC: Duke University Press.

Key Academic Text

Collins, Patricia Hill. 1998. *Fighting Words: Black Women and the Search for Justice*. Minneapolis: University of Minnesota Press.

Accessible Resource

Cappelle, Alice. 2022. "Tiime Is a Social Construct." https://www.youtube.com/watch?v=MV0CaXPteMs

References

Acker, Joan. 1990. "Hierarchies, Jobs, Bodies: A Theory of Gendered Organizations." *Gender and Society*, 4: 139–158.

Alakavuklar, Ozan Nadir, Dickson, Andrew G., and Stablein, Ralph. 2017. "The Alienation of Scholarship in Modern Business Schools: From Marxist Material Relations to the Lacanian Subject." *Academy of Management Learning and Education*, 16: 454–468.

Alinsky, Saul. 1971. *Rules for Radicals: A Pragmatic Primer for Realistic Radicals*. New York: Random House.

Baldwin, James. 1963/1993. *The Fire Next Time*. New York: Vintage Books.

Butler, Judith. 2005. *Giving an Account of Oneself.* New York: Fordham University Press.

Cockburn, Cynthia. 2015. "Transversal Politics: A Practice of Peace." *Pacific Feminism*, 22 February. https://www.icip.cat/perlapau/en/article/transversal-politics-a-practice-of-peace/?pdf.

Collins, Patricia H. 2013. "Truth-Telling and Intellectual Activism." *Contexts*, 12: 36–41.

Contu, Alessia. 2020. "Answering the Crisis with Intellectual Activism: Making a Difference as Business Schools Scholars." *Human Relations*, 73: 737–757.

Daniels, Norman. 1978. "Merit and Meritocracy." *Philosophy & Public Affairs*, 7: 206–223

Debord, Guy. 1967/2016. *Society of the Spectacle*. Detroit, MI: Black and Red.

Fisher, Mark. 2009. *Capitalist Realism: Is There No Alternative?* Winchester: Zero Books.

Freire, Paulo. 1994. *The Pedagogy of Hope*. London: Bloomsbury.

Giroux, Henry A. 2014. *Neoliberalism's War on Higher Education.* Chicago, IL: Haymarket Books.

Holvino, Evangelina. 2010. "Intersections: The Simultaneity of Race, Gender and Class in Organization Studies." *Gender, Work & Organization*, 17: 248–277.

hooks, bell. 1994. *Teaching to Transgress: Education as the Practice of Freedom*. New York: Routledge.

Lamberti, Raffaella. 2019. "Produzione di Politica Mediante Politica." https://women.it/wp-content/uploads/2019/11/ProduzioneDiPoliticaMediantePolitica.pdf.

Landes, David S. 1969. *The Unbound Prometheus: Technological Change and Industrial Development in Western Europe from 1750 to the Present.* Cambridge: Cambridge University Press.

Love, Bettina L. 2020. "An Essay for Teachers Who Understand Racism Is Real." *Education Week*. https://www-edweek-org.eu1.proxy.openathens.net/leadership/opinion-an-essay-for-teachers-who-understand-racism-is-real/2020/06.

Muller, Jerry Z. 2018. *The Tyranny of Metrics*. Princeton, NJ: Princeton University Press.

Muzanenhamo, Penelope, and Chowdhury, Rashedur. 2023. "Epistemic Injustice and Hegemonic Ordeal in Management and Organization Studies: Advancing Black Scholarship." *Human Relations*, 76: 3–26.

Nyberg, Daniel, Wright, Christopher, and Bowden, Vanessa. 2023. *Organising Responses to Climate Change: The Politics of Mitigation, Adaptation and Suffering.* Cambridge: Cambridge University Press.

Peredo, Ana Maria. 2023. "Indigenous and Divergent Voices in the Business School: Who's Listening?" *Management International*, 26: 144–148.

Sennett, Richard, and Cobb, Jonathan. 1972. *The Hidden Injury of Class.* London: Verso

Smith, Katherine E., Bandola-Gill, Justyna, Meer, Nasar, Stewart, Ellen A. and Watermeyer, Richard. 2020. *The Impact Agenda: Controversies, Consequences and Challenges.* Bristol: Policy Press.

Tallberg, Linda, and Hamilton, Lindsay. 2022. "Editors' Introduction." In *Oxford Handbook of Animal Organization Studies*, edited by Linda Tallberg and Lindsay Hamilton, 1–14. Oxford: Oxford University Press.

Young, Michael. 1959. The Rise of Meritocracy. New York: Random House.

Yuval-Davis, Nira. 1999. "What Is Transversal Politics?" *Soundings*, 12: 94–98.

4 Becoming Response-able Together in Research Fieldwork

Leni Grünbaum and Alice Wickström

A Beginning

The importance of response-ability—our embodied ability to respond to others—is becoming increasingly recognized in research practice. It is often seen as a ground for other-oriented engagements premised on relationality, openness, and vulnerability rather than normative ethical frameworks and principles (Hancock 2008; Johansson and Wickström, 2023; Pullen and Rhodes 2014, 2015). Scholars in management and organization have directed attention to how embodied encounters in the field (e.g., Dale and Latham 2015; Huber and Knights 2023; Mandalaki and Pérezts 2022) can promote knowledge rooted in generosity, reciprocity, and care. The Spinozian idea of "affecting and being affected" can be understood as central to this line of thought. However, it is important to note that not all encounters enhance or diminish capabilities to act and that an embodied response does not carry ethical weight in itself. Neither is it, as noted by Thanem and Wallenberg (2015, 247), necessarily a matter of "crafting harmonious relations" by "minimizing difference" but about enhancing our individual and collective capacities to act across differences, which cannot be achieved through control, exploitation, and domination. In research practice, this involves exploring how response-ability may draw on an ongoing affective[1] attunement to others (Gherardi 2017, 2019; Gherardi and Cozza 2022) and examining the entangled material-discursive conditions that enable (un)ethical encounters to unfold (Kinnunen 2023; Meriläinen et al. 2022; Valtonen and Pullen 2021).

Concerning fieldwork, Gherardi (2019) argues that affective attunement is grounded in an "intentional disposition to affect and be affected" that allows one to "be with" (8) both human and nonhuman others. This concept is distinguished from affective "resonance" or "contagion," in which individuals may get caught up in affective intensities—that is, affective flows and circuits in motion. Instead, the emphasis is placed on *how* to engage in an other-oriented sense, making attunement an ontological, epistemological, and ethical matter. This aligns with Bozalek's (2021) consideration of how "being attentive" may allow one to cultivate response-able research practices based on

DOI: 10.4324/9781003452485-4

experimentation, play, curiosity, and accountability. Following Gherardi and Bozalek, one can understand response-ability as a means for contemplating how to affectively respond in the present moment when conducting research rather than relying merely on normative ethical frameworks. When reflecting on encounters in research fieldwork, Helin (2013) and Meriläinen and colleagues (2022) illustrate how responding to "others" and "otherness" requires that we linger on possible hesitations, difficulties, and questions instead of viewing these as obstacles to research practice and knowledge development.

In this chapter, we take this premise as our starting point and explore the role of response-ability in research fieldwork. More specifically, we seek to understand how shifts in affective intensities shape the relationship between researchers and practitioners, as well as their capacities to act. Building on materials from the immersive coaching process of a leadership team, we elaborate on how the researcher-coach and the team negotiated becoming "response-able-together" and how this supported the unfolding of collective leadership.[2] We trace the affective intensities during the process and linger on moments in which differences in, for instance, ideas, rhythms, priorities, and embodied abilities gave rise to uncertainty and vulnerability. This exploration allows us to illustrate how response-ability in research may nurture reciprocal relationships that emerge from tensions instead of being grounded in and/or privileging consensus and unity. Moreover, we argue that response-able research can support organizational processes and practices that enhance individual and collective capacities to act while counter-acting forms of affective contagion that may work in disciplining and diminishing ways (see Guschke et al. 2023).

Our chapter is structured as follows. We first provide a brief background of the research project and process. This is followed by an expressive vignette in two parts, connected by an interlude, that seeks to capture how affective intensities prevented and enabled moments of and shifts in response-ability between the researcher-coach and the team. We then discuss how affective attunement informs response-ability in fieldwork and, more specifically, how it can support recognition, acceptance, and capabilities to work across tensions related to priorities, restrictions in resources, and institutional pressures, to name a few. We further discuss the importance of considering how engagement *with* others may unfold in ways that "trouble" normative frameworks for conducting fieldwork related to, for example, separateness between researchers and practitioners.

An Illustration from the Field

Our field illustration is based on research materials (e.g., field notes, the participants' written reflections after each coaching session, and transcripts from interviews and coaching sessions) from an immersive coaching process with a leadership team. These materials were collected by the first author and are part of a larger study that follows the development of three teams within child psychiatry (hereafter referred to as "The Organization") at a Nordic university hospital. In this chapter, we focus on the leadership team. Empirically, the study consisted of longitudinal fieldwork that integrated a participatory approach (Heron and Reason 2008) with an affective ethnographic style of engagement (Gherardi 2019). The participatory approach served as the foundation for the coaching process, consisting of five sessions lasting 3.5 hours each, grounded in and proceeding according to the needs recognized by the team. The orientation followed the principles of good relational practice work, as described by Lambrechts et al. (2009):

> Changing is coengaging in generative practices. The focus is on possibilities and new opportunities. The joint action is going where the energy is. … The essence … is doing things together in such a quality way that all actors involved benefit from the practice.
>
> (46)

While this quote refers to consulting work, it aligns well with an affective ethnographic approach to research that emphasizes the centrality of affective attunement in nurturing embodied knowledge (Gherardi 2019; Gherardi and Cozza 2022). Fieldwork is then not about the researcher "being there" but rather about becoming one with the data—that is, affecting and being affected by it (Gherardi 2019). In addition to the immersive coaching sessions, group interviews were conducted at the beginning and end of the process. The first author also shadowed individual team members during their everyday work.

The Organization and the Leadership Team

The Organization specializes in treating children with severe emotional and behavioral disorders and supporting their families. Its leadership team consists of eight members: five head psychiatrists, a senior nurse, a senior psychologist, and a senior social worker. The Organization is facing multiple challenges. The number of referrals has approximately doubled over the last decade, although costs are expected to be cut yearly. Recruiting psychiatrists, nurses, and other professionals has also become increasingly difficult. In response to the ensuing demands for effectiveness, the team has undertaken efforts to standardize the processes for diagnosing and treating patients, advance new forms of group care, and gather data to support decision-making and employee well-being. While these measures have allowed for catering to more patients, they have also generated tensions regarding, for example, who is entitled to care and for how long.

Since 2016, the first author has been coaching the team and its individual members, addressing issues ranging from coordination to crisis situations through pausing, embodied exploration, and reflexive sensemaking as means to move forward. In 2019, the team initiated a restructuring to manage the shortage of psychiatrists, which increased the workload for team members. Later that year, the hospital transitioned to a new patient information system that involved extensive coordination, learning, and support. This process was still ongoing in the spring of 2020, when the COVID-19 pandemic required The Organization to urgently develop remote care capabilities and impose stringent restrictions that isolated employees from one another. During this time, the researcher-coach and the team agreed to conduct the study, whose initial focus was on meaningful encounters between organizational members and the role of such encounters in seeking direction and enhancing collaboration.

After concluding her final session as a paid coach in May 2020, the first author transitioned from her role as a professional coach to that of a researcher-coach. Fieldwork began in April 2021 with remote group interviews. While everyday work continued, the future loomed blurry and uncertain: the national healthcare system was being restructured, and the change would alter the role of The Organization and its relations with the other actors in the field. Amid this upheaval, the team needed to redefine the purpose of The Organization, facing not only professional and organizational issues but also political and broad societal questions about the structure of child psychiatry, stakeholder collaboration, and The Organization's role in the evolving landscape.

Threading Encounters

To explore response-ability and affective attunement in fieldwork, the first author began by mapping out encounters from the coaching sessions that had stood out for her and the team members. By being attentive to how the participants engaged in and reflected on the sessions, she aimed to recognize shifts in affective intensities during the process. In this way, she sought to tease out the "material traces" (Gherardi and Cozza 2022) of affect and how they had come to animate the coaching process. This mapping generated a series of encounters whose affective intensities were described amply by both the team members (in their reflections) and the first author (in her field notes). Alongside these materials, the first author used video recordings and transcripts from the sessions to gain a better understanding of the events. Inspired by Stewart's (2007) work, she then sketched a vignette in two parts brought together by a short interlude. The vignette is a combination of the first author's ethnographic field notes and storytelling, and it is meant to convey how the affective intensities prevented and enabled moments of and shifts in response-ability between the researcher-coach and the team.

When writing up the vignette, the first author tried to be faithful to the multiplicity and unpredictability that marked the encounters and the affective intensities that made them stand out (Gherardi 2019; Hunter and Kivinen 2023). She refrained from outlining direct correlations between happenings and from fixating meanings through representational analysis. The aim was rather, in Stewart's (2007) words, to "provoke attention to the forces that come into view as habit or shock, resonance or impact. Something throws itself in a moment as an event and a sensation; a something both animated and inhabitable" (1). In practice, the writing proceeded slowly as an entanglement of narrating and affectively reliving the situations and sentiments. The first author then shared the vignettes with the second author, and they engaged in exploratory discussions to dwell on and sharpen the affective movement of the text. Hopefully, the vignette will allow for an affective understanding of the coaching process and its complexities by inviting forth an "actively passive" reading in which the words (and, importantly, the spaces between them) resonate in the world of the reader (Gherardi 2023). With this aim, the affective intensities have been highlighted in italics. For the sake of clarity, "she" and "her" refer to the researcher-coach, while the team members are referred to by name. With this, the reader is invited to join the researcher-coach and the team in their first session.

Becoming "Response-able Together"

First Encounter

> Needs are unpredictable. They may enter a room in bundles, and you don't realize how much space they take until you find yourself squeezed by their presence.
>
> They meet on the fourth floor. This grey September afternoon, five out of eight are there. Livia is ill, Lila is on research leave, and Anneli will join them later. A reunion after 12 months of lockdown. *Giggles and a bubbling sense hover around the bossy conference table.* The chatting meanders from Covid-19 vaccinations to the patient system, HR, yesterday's project meeting, and the countless burdening issues to be addressed. They start with a check-in: taking turns, each person stretches according to their need, and the others follow their example, then each one shares how they feel about the process. Janie is open to whatever will come. Vera feels the hyperactivity in her body, pausing has been impossible for some time. Anika wonders whether she has the energy for one more developmental effort. *There seems to too much of everything and no time to stop or to be present.* Will they be able to change anything? The coach listens in.
>
> Today, they need to agree on a focus for the process. To her earlier request, they came up with three: acting systematically, time management and scheduling, and well-being and collaboration in leadership. *A tall order.* She shows the topics and invites them to talk and listen to each other. What do they wish to get out of the process? Eight more topics emerge, big

and small but mostly big: 'purpose' and 'vision'. Astonishment: they are very different from the initial ones and from the issues brought up in the interviews! Henrietta laughs "That was then". Anika explains breathlessly "This is our reality, in every unit we are everywhere all at once". *A feast with too many dishes to choose from and more being carried to the table by the minute. The energy is perky yet somehow unsettling.* She feels lonely and insufficient, rummaging through her imagination for a helpful handle.

Anneli joins them through Teams. Her face is blank, her voice contained and toneless. Anneli's closest colleague will remain on sick leave for one more month, and Anneli will be doing the work of two: "My goal and my wish is to survive, one day at a time". Anika cups her hands in the shape of a heart. The system is unsustainable; *one of them at death's door all the while.* Vera confesses having been close to tears just yesterday, wondering how to cope. They don't have enough physicians and nurses, and maybe this is the new normal? *Catastrophes just keep on occurring.* How can they even stay focused on the big picture? She tries to make space but it feels as they were running uphill. *The forces circulating in the room have a foul stickiness.* They need a clearing. She suggests they map all possible topics under the three initial headings. Maybe it will bring a sense of distance and calm? They write in silence and then share their thoughts in pairs. The Jamboard document receives 20 more issues, escorted by agitation and jittery discussions. *The room shrinks and a sense of hyperactivity lingers.* She feels herself cramping. Anika notes that this is nothing compared to their usual state of mind. She hopes that an embodied activity will allow them to ground and reconnect. They start clapping their hands one at a time, looking at one another. *The atmosphere settles a bit.* Afterward, each person indicates their preferred topic, and the researcher-coach marks it with their initials. Next time, they will continue from there. Later, she feels tired, perplexed, and clueless. What needs to be addressed? The decision is theirs, but deciding seems difficult.

The session takes place in a conference room with scarce space to move. The beginning is marked by the warmth of reunion and the participants' different orientations, embodied abilities, and rhythms: openness and skepticism, bodily tension, and an impossibility to pause, among others. The researcher-coach listens in, trusting that recognizing and articulating differences will help engage with the shared task of selecting a focus—necessary for a purposeful process. However, affective flows are unpredictable: the "too much of everything" travels into the session, materializing in innumerable new needs and wishes and an upbeat energy inaccessible to the researcher-coach. Her feelings of loneliness and insufficiency signal that differences are not being recognized; her efforts to advance the shared process do not yield a (hoped-for) response. Nevertheless, loneliness and insufficiency mark the participants' experience, too; hence, hers could indicate that she is attuned to the affective circuits in the room. For her, the session brought more questions than answers. In the cramped space of the session, choosing a focus to produce direction for the process proved impossible. Did the session create a helpful space for co-action? Did it enhance their capacities to act? Hardly so.

Interlude

> Intensities come together sneakily. One day, you find yourself caught up in an unwanted flow. Amid discomfort, you reluctantly come to understand: simply getting back to business is not an option.
>
> During the following weeks, she tries to find a room where they can use the space freely. *They need material circumstances that support movement and a sense of possibility!* She mails them: could they come to the university's premises? The days pass, then a week: a reminder and another one. Finally, Livia asks them to respond. In the meantime, she has sent them an update: they can use the hospital's lecturing hall. Days later, reactions to her initial inquiry start dropping in, and another mail exchange is needed to sort things out. *A gnawing frustration.* In parallel, she has been chasing one of them for weeks to resolve a central matter agreed upon. To her emails, text messages, and phone calls, all she gets is silence. She cannot continue working with them in this state, *lost in feelings of worthlessness and shame, anger and exhaustion.* Then she realizes her emotions are information. Perhaps, others in the organization feel just like she does? She needs to bring this up! The insight comes with relief, fear, and a sense of anticipation so dense that she starts talking to herself as if she were talking to them.

The affective flows of the first session have an afterlife in which affective attunement and affective contagion complicate one another. What started as "an intentional disposition to affect" the process "and be affected" by it (Gherardi 2019, 8) has transformed into something else. The researcher-coach is caught in an affective circuit whose power makes her question her capacity to act with the team altogether. What is clear is that to "notice how she notices," she needs to open herself to the affective, embodied experience. Luckily, there is enough time-space for doing so before the next session and for finding the courage to confront the team with her new affective understanding.

Second Encounter

> New worlds don't always surrender to plans. For example: you might discern the contours of an intention and decide to act on it. From there, you have no choice but to move along and find out what is about to take shape.
>
> Before the second session, tension travels through her body. They meet in the lecturing hall of the hospital. *Finally, plenty of space to move.*

Today everyone will attend. *Hilarious chitchatting floats in the room.* Though she nervously struggles with the screen and they start late, the good mood persists. The check-in is paced with liberating laughter, and they throw themselves into pair work to shake off unnecessary burdens. *Thrilling.* The previous session evokes rich reflections. Henrietta says it felt good to belong to this group. It was valuable to be present, to receive Anneli's emotion, and to recognize it in oneself and each other. And yet, this is only work. Taking four hours to meet like this, well… It won't make this house of cards crash. Livia lifts her hands as if holding up the roof. *The room echoes with deep chortles.* Ramona says sharing is crucial "because once you share things, you can go forward". Softly, Janie says "belonging is what we should promote and foster now". Perhaps trying to solve things is not always the best thing to do? Could they just note how things are, and learn to tolerate and stay with that discomfort? Lila says: "What can one do in the face of the impossible?".

It is time for 'observations from the researcher-coach'. With cheeks burning, she says she knows them as competent and responsible, kind and constructive. Together, they are entwined in this process and so, she uses herself as a research instrument. She's been struck by her emotional reactions, countertransference one could call it. Their discussions often yield joy and enthusiasm, but there's another story as well. The mail exchanges invoke frustration, anger, and tiredness. Not receiving any responses suggests that participating in the study is unimportant, evoking *shame*. Sure, it makes interesting data but in The Organization such episodes could erode the trust of employees towards those at the top. She does not mean to blame them, simply to hold up a mirror. And yes, there's something else too. Her deep insufficiency during the first session… *A sense of hesitation.* Could it have been both mine and yours? Is focusing on one thing impossible because it would mean ignoring everything else? She invites them to share their thoughts with a colleague. *The thick silence melts into animated conversations, harboring a sense of release.* Feeling bare and a bit dizzy, she sees herself having stood by a steep precipice. *The ravine was there all right, but she didn't fall into it.* Where is this going?

The sharing takes off, forming ties of recognition across the room. Her reflection seems to have stopped them right in their tracks, now giving rise to affirmative attention. "You described well what emotions not responding to each other can lead to… And what kind of atmosphere does one then contribute to create?", Henrietta reflects openly. At the same time, new demands keep on coming: from outside the organization, the patients, their teams, and admin. To cope, they must narrow themselves down. "This is such a big vessel, and we're a terribly small crowd.", Anika notes. Each and everyone of them would need to be split into three! Vera is tired of being nice to everyone. Livia says that one needs to be nasty at times too. She mentions her wonder while shadowing Janie. Despite the many twists and turns, Janie was sharp and managed to take in the big picture, all while listening to those around her. *How was it possible?* Returning to the house of cards, maybe they cannot hold up all the walls all the time? Maybe they need to pause and carve out some space for themselves too? *To find ways of not renouncing themselves for work yet to feel at peace.*

The lecture hall is spacious, allowing the chairs to be arranged freely and for work to be done sitting or standing. With time, the affective circuits of the first encounter come to nurture warm humor, merciful reflection, and suggestions. Perhaps it did act as a space for collaboration, after all, enhancing the capacities of the team members? From here, a new affective intensity builds up as the researcher-coach shares her observations and vulnerability. This critical juncture fosters not only recognition of her experience but also personal contemplation and difference: despite similarities, theirs come with distinctive flavors, emphases, and insights. Accepting and affirming both the collective and the individual creates a new space for co-action where well-being can be explored in an open-ended way. Marked by connection and anchoring, the affective flow thus enhances the team's capacity to act. Through the laborious and unpredictable untangling of humans, priorities, limited resources, and institutional pressures for effectiveness, an affective space emerges where the team can take the next crucial step in a constructive direction.

A Continuation

In this chapter, we set out to explore the role of response-ability in research fieldwork. More specifically, we consider how an emphasis on affective attunement (Gherardi 2019) can allow us to understand how individual and collective capacities to act in other-oriented ways (e.g., Helin 2013; Johansson and Wickström 2023; Meriläinen et al. 2022) are both enabled and hindered. Drawing on materials from an immersive coaching process, we traced the affective intensities of the process through a twofold vignette and examined the possibilities for the researcher-coach and the team to become "response-able together." In what follows, we revisit some key moments from the encounters and elaborate on how we can understand them through the lens of response-ability.

In the first part of the vignette, we find the researcher-coach and team struggling to collectively orient toward a focus for the process. Along with doubt about yet another developmental effort, there are simply too many "dishes" on the table. Anneli embodies the personal and interpersonal effects of their workload and the others recognize themselves in her experience. The moment underscores the experience of chaos, thus adding to the affective density. Untangling is necessary, yet merely externalizing the topics does not lessen the affective intensity. On the contrary, a sense of hyperactivity seems to impede attentiveness to anything else. While an embodied exercise allows them to relate to one another differently and brings some composure, the situation and the focus of the process remain unresolved. The myriad affective flows seem to prevent the team members from attuning and thus responding to their shared difficulties. Nevertheless, in their reflections, some participants noted how sharing their emotional burdens and recognizing themselves in others' struggles brought a sense of relief.

The interlude bridges the first and second sessions by tracing the researcher-coach's affective journey between the two, highlighting that the affective flows of the process do not cease. Instead, the intensity grows week by week until she sees no alternative to confronting the team with her affective observations.

In the second session, we are met with a sense of ease among the participants, evident in light energies and vibrant chitchat. However, the atmosphere soon shifts as the researcher-coach shares her affective insights. In doing so, she steps away from being an objective researcher, detached from the context. By revealing her vulnerability, she risks losing her credibility and their respect. However, they will not be able to move forward together unless she voices the affective flows that shape their relationships. Her sharing evokes not only surprise and guilt but also satisfaction as emotions are articulated and recognized. This encourages team members to acknowledge the researcher-coach's needs and to act more response-ably toward both themselves and one another by sharing their own experiences and struggles. Instead of being engulfed by the affective flow, the conversation comes across as open, grounded, and nuanced. In pairs, they affirm their relationship to well-being and acknowledge differences, thereby strengthening their connections. Through these new ways of relating, new possibilities begin to take shape.

A thread emerges between the encounters as attempts to respond across differences give rise to uncertainties, vulnerabilities, and, thus, tensions. Despite efforts to produce an articulated direction for the process, affective flows first orient the team and the researcher-coach elsewhere, hindering an adequate space for co-action from emerging. Toward the end, something shifts, bringing a sense of ease and room to breathe, perhaps allowing for the possibility of becoming "response-able together" instead of simply reacting.

How to Become Response-able Together?

The story we have told is one of many possible stories that could have been told. In what ways can it add to our understanding of affective attunement and response-ability in research fieldwork? First, the team had been in a challenging situation for years but had, nonetheless, been able to function competently and take its work forward in significant ways. Collectively, the team members thus stand out as having the capacity to move between contexts and to contain frustration and burdening emotions. Additionally, the story suggests that they can recognize and receive emotions. Thus, once they lived through the affective release of the first session, they found their way back from engulfing affective flows and engaged in reflection, which helped them move forward. Indeed, capacities to act must always be understood as contextual, situated, and relational.

How can affective attunement then support response-able research? While Gherardi (2019) emphasizes that affective attunement can entail relations with both human and nonhuman others, our focus is on social relations in research fieldwork. Our story suggests that by affirming our relations with the other humans involved, affective attunement creates opportunities for recognition, reciprocity, and responsiveness. The relational space is inhabited not only by the humans but also by priorities and possible foci for the process, experiences and emotions, past events, and metaphors. Through a sense of affective attunement, one can examine how one relates to these elements, untangle possible tensions within a relational space, and thus support other-oriented, response-able engagement. However, a focus on response-ability troubles research, and as our story suggests, there is no definite recipe. Openness is key: we try something, then we try something else. All the while, we try to attune to how affective intensities unfold, using them as "clues" to explore and learn from rather than simply reacting to them. In this way, they might inform us about the organizations, groups, and phenomena we study and, more specifically, what it is like to "be" in and with them, and about ourselves. While such other-oriented engagement involves uncertainty and vulnerability, we are short of options: one can arguably not become response-able without putting oneself in a disposition of affective attunement.

We would also like to note that affective attunement should not be reduced to a normative ethical ideal for conducting fieldwork. An emphasis on "should" could here orient attention, practices, and energies in ways that privilege the possible outcome of being attuned or acting response-ably. This might form a hindrance to staying present—and thus open to whatever trouble is to come—by turning attunement into a goal rather than a means. On the contrary, we believe that affective attunement in fieldwork is best furthered through embodied explorations (Bozalek 2021), for example, by sensitizing oneself to affective intensities by recognizing silences, tensions, and difficulties; by orienting toward the verbal and embodied language of the participants; and by making and taking time to let things happen and to linger on the process individually and in different constellations. Essentially, this approach involves not only talking about but also "living with" our fieldwork and its open-endedness.

Recommended Reading

Original Text by Donna Haraway

Haraway, Donna J. *Staying with the Trouble: Making Kin in the Chthulucene*. New York: Duke University Press, 2016.

Key Academic Text

Pors, Justine Grønbæk. "The Political and Ethical Potential of Affective Resonance between Bodies." In *Diversity, Affect and Embodiment in Organizing*, edited by Marianna Fotaki and Alison Pullen, 23–46. Cham: Palgrave Macmillan, 2018.

Accessible Resource

Then & Now. Human(itie)s, in context, "Introduction to Affect Theory: Brian Massumi & Eve Sedgwick", accessed June 26th, 2024. https://www.thenandnow.co/2023/06/15/introduction-to-affect-theory-brian-massumi-eve-sedgwick/

Notes

1 Affect is here understood as intensities that emerge between human and nonhuman bodies and shape organizational embodiments, encounters, and interactions beyond the rational and representational (Fotaki et al. 2017; Hunter and Kivinen 2023).

2 The latter is here defined as a situated, relational, and "ongoing process signifying the pursuit of direction in the production of a space for co-action" (Sklaveniti 2020, 73) in which direction is constructed moment by moment and space refers to the way relating unfolds.

References

Bozalek, Vivienne. "Rendering Each Other Capable: Doing Response-able Research Responsibly." In *Navigating the Postqualitative, New Materialist and Critical Posthumanist Terrain Across Disciplines*, edited by Karin Murris, 135–149. New York: Routledge, 2021.

Dale, Karen, and Yvonne Latham. "Ethics and Entangled Embodiment: Bodies–Materialities–Organization." *Organization* 22, no. 2 (2015): 166–182.

Fotaki, Marianna, Kate Kenny, and Sheena Vachhani. "Thinking Critically about Affect in Organization Studies: Why It Matters." *Organization* 24, no. 1 (2017): 3–17.

Gherardi, Silvia. "Which Is the Place of Affect within Practice-Based Studies?" *M@n@gement* 20, no. 2 (2017): 208–220.

Gherardi, Silvia. "Theorizing Affective Ethnography for Organization Studies." *Organization* 26, no. 6 (2019): 741–760.

Gherardi, Silvia. "In the Worlding of Kathleen Stewart: Daydreaming a Conversation with 'SHE'." In *Affect in Organization and Management*, edited by Carolyn Hunter and Nina Kivinen, 29–44. New York: Routledge, 2023.

Gherardi, Silvia, and Michela Cozza. "Atmospheric Attunement in the Becoming of a Happy Object: 'That Special Gut Feeling'." In *Doing Process Research in Organizations: Noticing Differently*, edited by Barbara Simpson and Line Revabæk, 16–38. Oxford: Oxford University Press, 2022.

Guschke, Bontu Lucie, Jannick Friis Christensen, and Thomas Burø. "Sara Ahmed: A Return to Emotions." In *Affect in Organization and Management*, edited by Carolyn Hunter and Nina Kivinen, 12–28. New York: Routledge, 2023.

Hancock, Philip. "Embodied Generosity and an Ethics of Organization." *Organization Studies* 29, no. 10 (2008): 1357–1373.

Helin, Jenny. "Dialogic Listening: Toward an Embodied Understanding of How to 'Go On' during Fieldwork." *Qualitative Research in Organizations and Management: An International Journal* 8, no. 3 (2013): 224–241.

Heron, John, and Peter Reason. "Extending Epistemology within a Co-Operative Inquiry." In *The Sage Handbook of Action Research: Participative Inquiry and Practice*, edited by Peter Reason and Hilary Bradbury, 366–380. London: Sage, 2008.

Huber, Guy, and David Knights. "When 'I' Becomes 'We': An Ethnographic Study of Power and Responsibility in a Large Food Retail Cooperative." *Human Relations* 76, no. 8 (2023): 1137–1161.

Hunter, Carolyn, and Nina Kivinen. *Affect in Organization and Management*. New York: Routledge, 2023.

Johansson, Janet, and Alice Wickström. "Constructing a 'Different' Strength: A Feminist Exploration of Vulnerability, Ethical Agency and Care." *Journal of Business Ethics* 184, no. 2 (2023): 317–331.

Kinnunen, Vera. "Corporeal Ethics in the More-than-Human World." In *Affect in Organization and Management*, edited by Carolyn Hunter and Nina Kivinen, 92–107. New York: Routledge, 2023.

Lambrechts, Frank, Styn Grieten, René Bouwen, and Felix Corthouts. "Process Consultation Revisited: Taking a Relational Practice Perspective." *The Journal of Applied Behavioral Science* 45, no. 1 (2009): 39–58.

Mandalaki, Emmanouela, and Mar Pérezts. "It Takes Two to Tango: Theorizing Inter-Corporeality through Nakedness and Eros in Researching and Writing Organizations." *Organization* 29, no. 4 (2022): 596–618.

Meriläinen, Susan, Tarja Salmela, and Anu Valtonen. "Vulnerable Relational Knowing that Matters." *Gender, Work & Organization* 29, no. 1 (2022): 79–91.

Pullen, Alison, and Carl Rhodes. "Corporeal Ethics and the Politics of Resistance in Organizations." *Organization* 21, no. 6 (2014): 782–796.

Pullen, Alison, and Carl Rhodes. "Ethics, Embodiment and Organizations." *Organization* 22, no. 2 (2015): 159–165.

Sklaveniti, Chrysavgi. "Moments that Connect: Turning Points and the Becoming of Leadership." *Human Relations* 73, no. 4 (2020): 544–571.

Stewart, Kathleen. *Ordinary Affects*. Durham: Duke University Press, 2007.

Thanem, Torkild, and Louise Wallenberg. "What Can Bodies Do? Reading Spinoza for an Affective Ethics of Organizational Life." *Organization* 22, no. 2 (2015): 235–250.

Valtonen, Anu, and Alison Pullen. "Writing with Rocks." *Gender, Work & Organization* 28, no. 2 (2021): 506–522.

5 Playing with Theatre in Research Practices

Response-ability and *Becoming with* a Queer Community

Carmen Pellegrinelli and Laura Lucia Parolin

Introduction

This chapter intends to contribute to the debate about response-ability as a necessary capacity in research practices. The research focuses on the relationship between queerness and response-ability using arts as a tool of inquiry. In this contribution, we conceptualize response-ability as a form of *becoming with* of queer community members and researchers, which is mobilized by the material and affective forces of the theatrical performance. We focus on how these forces affect the queer communities involved in the research and their subjectivity, as well as us as researchers. Considering response-ability in our research practices implies thinking about our position as queer researchers embodying an ethical posture to understand how research influences our queer and professional identities.

Our interest in investigating queer subjectivities through the lens of affect emerged in our activities as activists in the LGBTQIA+ community. For a few years (2007–2014), we ran a lesbian association in a small space in the centre of Milan, where readings, small concerts, theatre workshops, and book presentations were often organized. In those days, we had the opportunity to experience the community as a safe place to develop a solid sense of self that was not threatened and diminished, as often happens to queer subjectivities in Italy. We had, therefore, the opportunity to *become with* our queer companions.

Our research interest builds on our experiences as activists and focuses on how we *become with* the queer communities we still inhabit. As Eleanor Formby (2017) states, there are many ways to understand the "LGBTQIA+ community" concept. We opt for a performative definition of the LGBTQIA+ community rather than an ostensive one. We understand the community not as a fixed entity but as something that emerges from the daily social practices of LGBTQIA+ people. In our case, discussing books, movies, TV series, and play theatre and talking about our life experiences were a way to produce

DOI: 10.4324/9781003452485-5

community. A community that can be conceptualized as an emerging place of subjectivity affirmation where LGBTQIA+ people *become together*.

By mobilizing the Spinozian-Deleuzian affect literature (Massumi 2015) and affirmative ethics (Braidotti 2019), we investigate how *becoming with* within the safe space of a community consists of a process of mirroring and recognition between LGBTQIA+ subjectivities that foster mutual affirmation and reciprocal becoming. Following Johnston (2016), we agree that affirmation is a form of healing that helps queer subjectivities flourish. In this chapter, we highlight how this act of caring (often) occurs in LGBTQIA+ communities through the projection of a gaze of kindness (Haraway 2015) on others. This allows an affective resonance that makes it possible for multiple subjectivities to express themselves.

From this perspective, we aim to contribute to the discussion on response-ability as a process of affective mirroring that mobilizes affirmative ethics and allows subjectivities to express and become in the richness of their potential. In the discussion, we elaborate on how we *became with* LGBTQIA+ activists in the research we conducted.

For our research, we decided to use art-based methods, particularly theatre, to provoke and stimulate new knowledge, according to a non-representational onto-epistemological approach. Arts and artistic methods are precious for social research because they allow experimenting with spaces and rules of everyday life (Gherardi 2019). Therefore, to explore the collective processes of becoming in relation to LGBTQIA+ subjectivity, we used a queer theatre performance to engage a small group of Italian LGBTQIA+ activists.

The theatre play was crafted in the spring of 2023 by Carmen, one of the authors of this chapter, who, besides being a researcher, is also a professional playwright and theatre director. In March 2023, we set up a meeting with the preview of the play with a focus group for activists as a step toward constructing the play and investigating queerness through arts-based research methods. Two months after, the theatre play premiered at the queer festival Orlando in Bergamo (Italy). The theatre performance titled "Stone" is a monologue freely inspired[1] by Leslie Feinberg's novel *Stone Butch Blues* (1993). The book is the fictional biography of Jess Goldberg, who, between the 1960s and 1980s, lived facing the reality of not feeling like she belongs to either gender, but instead of embodying another, creative, and non-binary dimension, in continuous negotiation with the context and contact with the deepest self. The novel is a classic of LGBTQIA+ literature, translated into many languages. The 20th Anniversary Author's Edition (Feinberg 2014) is available at the author´s website: http://www.lesliefeinberg.net/. It also explores the history of the movements for the rights of trans, gay, and lesbian people in the USA, and it is still a very current text in tackling classism, racism, capitalism, homophobia, and transphobia.

Our motivation in approaching research with this art-based design entails multiple aspects. On a professional artistic level, Carmen needed to understand if the performance was working and reaching the audience. As activists, we wanted to understand what issues were most relevant to the LGBTQIA+ communities after several years of less active presence. Finally, as researchers, we wanted to understand if and how the affects mobilized in the performance resonated with the audience. We wanted to make empathic, physical, and embedded contact with the activists and experiment with theatre to stimulate their active and sensitive responses. We wanted to perceive the activists epidermally, referring to Barad (2007, 392), to have the activists in our skin.

Response-Ability and Queerness

According to Vivienne Bozalek and Zembylas Michalinos (2023), the concept of response-ability emerged in feminist new materialist conversation with the contributions of Karen Barad, Donna Haraway, and Vinciane Despret, along with Joan Tronto's work on political ethics of care.

Response-ability, as a concept, refers not only to the ability to respond but also to the capacity to enable and invite the response of others. To explore response-ability in LGBTQIA+ communities, we focus on rendering each other capable as a way to develop what Johnston (2016) calls "affirmation" as an act of care that makes LGBTQIA+ subjectivities flourish.

Rendering each other capable can be seen as an action of caring, where identities co-constitute and transform themselves in an ecological relationality (Bozalek and Michalinos 2023). From our own experience as queer activists, we can say that in LGBTQIA+ communities, the practice of enabling each other is widespread. LGBTQIA+ communities enable the practice of mutual recognition in which the identity paths of queer subjectivities are strengthened.

Therefore, we agree with Johnston (2016) that in their relationships, LGBTQIA+ people experiment with affirmation as an embodied phenomenon that determines the good quality of staying in and inhabiting a social context. According to Johnston (2016), the key element that allows LGBTQIA+ subjectivities to flourish and assert themselves is the network of relationships they engage in and the narrative that shapes their perception of themselves in relation to others.

Regarding relationships and self-expression, Rosi Braidotti (2019) talks about affirmative ethics. According to Braidotti (2019, 317), affirmative ethics is "a collective practice of constructing social horizons of hope, in response to the flagrant injustices, the perpetuation of old hierarchies and new forms of domination". With the concept of affirmative ethics, Braidotti invites the mobilization of potentialities, active forces of life to cultivate degrees of empowerment, and affirmation of one's interconnections with others in their multiplicity. Affirmative ethics is particularly helpful to queerness because it enables the ever-moving queer project that disassembles and reassembles elements in creative ways such as imagination, contestation, and disturbance.

Affirmative ethics is based on radical relationality, which aims to empower subjectivities by increasing their ability to relate to others in a productive and mutually reinforcing manner. In Braidotti's (2019, 167) words, the affirmative "ethics ideal is to increase one's ability to enter into a mode of relations with multiple others and to create a community that actualizes this ethical propensity".

One way to increase one's ability to enter a relational mode with multiple others consists of affectively projecting a look of kindness onto them. As Donna Haraway (2015) reminds us, Vinciane Despret discusses the cultivation of politeness as a particular epistemological position. The practice of politeness reflects on the other a glance of affective support, care, understanding, and esteem. Inside this glance, identity affirmation can emerge as a process that creates the relational self, reflecting and stabilizing an aspect of the self (Johnston 2016). This process of identity affirmation is not a cognitive or mental act but a practice of affective *attuning* that releases the energy of empowerment, recognition, and affirmation in the relationship.

We can consider the concept of attunement as closely related to affect. In the Spinozian-Deleuzian framework, affect is defined as the capacity of a body to affect and be affected. This can be related to attunement in terms of what happens in the immediacy of an event (Zourabichvili 2012). Massumi (2015) defines attunement as the direct capture of attention and energy by an event. In this sense, we can consider affective attunement as a practice that produces positive and joyful energy in the event of an encounter between bodies.

Therefore, an affective attunement practice cannot be carried only by human intentionality but must be felt by the bodies engaged in the relationship. For example, referring to our experiences as queer bodies, we claim that we can feel when someone is not comfortable in contact with us, even if he/she does not explicitly declare it. Feeling welcome or not as queer subjects and understanding it from the glance and the body of others is embodied knowledge among queer people, as well as other minorities. Affective attuning through the practice of politeness, thus, cannot be displayed based on human intentionality, and it requires acts of caring as an affective force that mobilizes intellectual resources like:

The ability to find others actively interesting, even or especially others most people already claim to know all too completely, to ask questions that one's interlocutors truly find interesting, to cultivate the wild virtue of curiosity, to retune one's ability to sense and respond – and to do all this politely (Haraway 2015, 5).

Thus, the practice of politeness is at the core of rendering each other capable of constructing a joyous queer community where multiple subjectivities can flourish. Considering queerness as a set of potentials not manifestly visible within the normed binary context, we can understand how rendering each other capable means making hidden potentials emerge and enabling multiple subjectivities. The queer community works as an antidote against the forces that ask LGBTQIA+ people to hide their "oddness".

Similarly to what happens in LGBTQIA+ communities, politeness and attunement toward a positive affirmation must be at the core of research practices when researching queerness. As Bozalek (2020) states, rendering each other capable in terms of research entails generating "experiments with" rather than "on" participants. Doing research "with" and not "on" queer people requires politeness to render each other capable and let the potentials that inhabit queerness manifest. It implies *becoming with* each other and learning from encounters without using pre-existing accounts. As Despret (2016) underlines, in this perspective, it is possible to reconfigure research apparatuses by making them performative and purposeful places.

Case and Methods

The case we propose is part of a project conducted by the authors to investigate LGBTQIA+ subjectivities in queer communities. The phenomenon of inquiry is the reception of the LGBTQIA+ theatre play written and directed by one of the authors. Specifically, in this contribution, we analyze the materials that emerged/were co-produced in a focus group with representatives of the queer community who attended the viewing of a fragment of the play before its debut at the queer festival Orlando in Bergamo (Italy). The one-hour play is a monologue inspired by Feinberg's book described above and performed by the non-binary actor Laura M. The fragment of the play lasted about 30 minutes and was a preparatory study of the whole play. The performance, followed by the focus group, was presented in a hall of a municipal space dedicated to young people for events, training, performances, music, and coworking.

As we mentioned, the audience participating in the focus group comprised members of various Italian LGBTQIA+ associations. We limited the performance and the focus group to activists. The idea was to engage in a conversation and invite the response of people who are very sensitive to the topic and used to engage in mutual relationships with the social environment. The occasion arrived with a national meeting of the Italian National Feminist Lesbian Association (ALFI) in Bergamo. Therefore, many of the audience consisted of ALFI representatives from different cities. ALFI was founded in 2018 by people from ArciLesbica, unsatisfied by the national management of the historic lesbian association accused of being transphobic. ALFI aims to fight discrimination against lesbian, bisexual, transgender and intersex women, and any LGBTQIA+ person. We are members of ALFI Bergamo, the local association hosting the national meeting. Thus, we proposed the performance and the focus group as a side activity for the meeting, inviting other local activists. Among them, there were promoters and activists of the Bergamo queer festival Orlando, a plural, intersectional, and cross-disciplinary festival that has been animating the city of Bergamo for ten years (2014-present), hosting international artists, and creating a transversal community that works on queerness. Moreover, there were members of the group coalited around organizing the local annual Pride parade, and Rete Lenford, a national lawyer association fighting for LGBTQIA+ rights, with headquarters in Bergamo.

The performance started at 7 p.m. when the sun was still shining. The room was not a theatre hall but a narrow, grey meeting room with a long, darkened window on one side. Despite the technical difficulties, the space was adapted to the needs of the stage by darkening part of the window and installing spotlights. The space was used longitudinally, with the stage at one end of the room and the audience seated on chairs at the front.

The fragment performed was inspired by the first part of the *Stone Butch Blues* novel. It consisted of an opening scene presenting Jess's problem – Jess is the novel's protagonist – her (she uses the "she" pronoun) struggle to find a place within the male/female binary system and her parents' rejection. The performance continued by showing Jess's first entry into a lesbian bar as an adolescent, her happy discovery of the community, and her first experience with a police raid on the lesbian bar she frequented. In prison, Jess witnesses police violence against her fellow prisoners. Then, the story continued with Jess's sexual assault by schoolmates and her consequent dropping out of school. Finally, the story follows Jess's entrance into the lesbian and trans community before she is arrested and raped by the police. The embrace and support of trans friends in the community and the first discovery of lesbian affection in a night of love with a lesbian femme concluded the fragment of the performance presented.

To carry out our research, we performed an affective ethnography (Pellegrinelli and Parolin 2023) and audio-recorded the focus group. We took a collaborative diary of the day, "writing down" affects, impressions, sensations, feelings, and expectations. We worked on the recordings of the conversation and carried out content analysis. In analyzing the materials that emerged from the encounter with the activists, we paid attention to affective atmospheres (Anderson 2009), trying to see how activists' bodies responded to the performance. In the following, we present some traces that emerged from activists' bodies, their affects, and their sensitive, emphatic responses.

Becoming with the Performance

During and after the performance, the group experiences an intense, strong, participatory affective atmosphere. From the very beginning of the focus group, the performance generated layers of intensity, images, emotions, experiences, memories, and stories among the activists. They state and demonstrate that they empathized with Jess through their bodies during the performance. However, the raw depiction of violence places the audience in an unreconciled position, at the centre of a hostile and unfriendly gaze that is one of their/our greatest fears. After a long and moving applause for Laura M., who played Jess, the focus group begins in a charged and silent atmosphere; like the lightning described by Barad and Gandorfer (2021), the energy accumulated during the performance had to be released.

In this first part of the focus group, several themes emerge concerning queer affirmation in a hostile social context and the need for a community as a safe place for queer personal development. Therefore, the response of the activists' bodies, made possible by the performance, is expressed in words through two significant themes: *violence* and *queer community*.

Excerpt 1

ALFI Activist 1: What struck me was the crude violence, as it were, that we witnessed, which personally does not leave me indifferent at all and even now, I am not […] I feel a bit with a delicate stomach, so maybe it's a direct approach. That's something that immediately enters a little bit…

In addition to the piece that emphasizes the activist's embodied response with her belly, other ALFI activists report having had an intense and painful experience witnessing Jess' story in the performance. Specifically, they state that they were struck and frightened by the depiction of violence. One activist states that the repeated acts of violence in the performance were excessive and made her nervous. Another one reports how the performance perfectly mirrored the atmosphere she experienced reading the novel. Therefore, she points out that it is the novel itself that has this kind of violent content.

The first reactions and testimonies on the theme of violence are very emotional and respond empathetically to Jess's experiences in a hostile world. These responses express an embodied reaction, communicating unease, fear, and inability to cope with violence and despair.

Then, slowly, the discomfort of exposure to violence is processed by the group collectively, and the activists begin to express a less desperate and more active reaction. Some of them began to talk about their relationship with anger as a form of response to violence. The performance stirs an emotional response to the desire for justice and the need for queer people to be respected. Common is the recognition that the reaction to this state of affairs towards restoring social justice also passes through the dimension of anger.

Excerpt 2

ALFI Activist 2: […] I had like a flash of lightning when there was the moment of the rape next to the football field where the protagonist, almost laughing, dramatically says: "But how? In the end, is the heterosexual love relationship this thing here?" [Quoting Jess thought during her rape] […]. For 90, 95 per cent of people, the sexual act is actually a predatory act. It is an act of overpowering. It is an act that sanctions and legitimises and eternalises a relationship of asymmetry [...] something violent and non-empathic, colonial and predatory, that is, as if the body of the other is a territory to be violated and not as an entity with which to enter into harmony, empathy, symbiosis [...] For us, not CIS people, this violence is somewhat the order of the day.

In the passage just presented, the activist recognizes herself in Jess's comment on the heteronormative sexual act. The activist expresses her point of view, which frames most heteronormative sexual acts as predatory. Her statement is echoed by another activist who decisively and passionately underlines the need to use violence to defend oneself from violence. This comment does not arouse any further reactions, and after the expression of a very warm point of view on the topic, the group returns to reflection in a calmer manner.

Examples of activists' lives are provided regarding the issue of violence against queer people. It is noted that violence is still present today, albeit less evidently. Some (gay) activists point out that they feel privileged not to suffer the violence Jess suffered. Other (lesbian) activists point out how violence is still intertwined with the issue of security today. An ALFI activist talks about the unpleasant episode of a public lesbian party in which a group of adult heterosexual males wanted to participate at all costs without respecting the activists' desire to organize a party reserved only for lesbians or queers. Although the incident did not lead to any evident episode of violence, the activists underline how they experienced it as dangerous and highly stressful. Furthermore, it emerges from the conversation that violence does not only consist in being beaten and raped but also of everyday abuse.

Excerpts 3

Orlando Activist 1: [...] I'm saying that violence, unfortunately, in my opinion, is still there because I bring my example. I work in a psychiatric community where there is a young person who has been telling the whole group for a year and more that he feels like a man. Yet, for a year and more, almost everyone still calls him feminine.

Parallel to the theme of violence, a second important topic that emerges in the focus group is the importance of the *queer community* as a place of protection from violence and as a pleasant space for self-affirmation. The advantages of belonging to a queer group emerge in the activists' conversation.

For example, the first comment in the focus group was about the scene where Jess enters a lesbian bar for the first time. Activists recognize Jess' entry into the community as an essential moment experienced by all in the development of queer subjectivity. They prove to be mirrored in Jess's feelings, but this time, this mirroring is pleasant, warm, and funny and develops a shared sense of comfort. A feeling that is also what unites people from different groups within the small focus group community.

Excerpts 4

ALFI Activist 3: [...] I was really struck by the situation of excitement, fear, and embarrassment in the first scene when she enters a lesbian club for the first time. I don't know; I really identified with that scene. The movements and the feeling it conveyed is something I also experienced, and I felt it very much. It was realistic, alive, and with many feelings that were not expressed. But they are all there. Now I'm very heated so that it will be someone else speaking. Thank you.

The reflection continues on how Jess's community is a place of solid solidarity between the lesbian world and trans women. In particular, concerning the scene in which Jess is welcomed, cared for and cuddled by her trans friends after the sexual violence by the police, in the focus group, the theme emerges through activists' comments on the community as a place of care and recognizing its role of being a chosen family (Weston 1997).

Excerpts 5

Orlando Activist 2: [...] I was very impressed by the solidarity between the protagonist and the trans-female world. [...] The cohesion and solidarity between these characters who appeared in the performance and that's something I've always liked, and I think it is fundamental.

In relation to the theme of care, a further reflection is raised on the relationship between the violent historical moment of the 1960s experienced by Jess and the cohesion of the communities in those years. The reflection opens the question of how cohesive communities are today and whether they are less so because there is less social pressure. This question then stimulates comments in recognizing elements of community coexistence even in the contemporary world. The care, affection, and recognition of others within small communities resonate in the personal memories of activists as an element of mutual empowerment and affirmation.

Excerpt 6

Orlando activist 3: I was very moved by the point where [Jess] talks about the two friends lifting her up as she feels the world is bringing her down. That touched me very, very much. I remembered all those times that there was some relationship, not so much community group relationship, because I always had small-group hangouts, but those few people who were the ones who lifted me up... who really gave me the push [...] I say to myself, maybe I could be the one to lift someone else, I don't know.

From this common emphasis on the care enacted by the community in today's world, the topic of protecting the community's youngest and most vulnerable members emerges. Here, the discussion shifts from the issue of protection to that of protection from violent content, underlining the need to protect the audiences from the content of the work presented. In other words, the activists highlight how the performative trigger offered by the researchers was emotionally intense and, therefore, needs to be rethought to contain and warn the audience of the violent contents of Jess' story.

Discussion

This research was particularly meaningful to us because it brought together three elements of our lives and work: activism, artistic, and academic work. As Barad[2] (2007) point out, knowing is a way of *becoming with* the world; it involves engaging in a conversation in which we open our multiple selves. Embracing the activist response-able posture means engaging in research ethically and responsibly and being willing to *become with* the research participants.

In the case we have presented and because our personal and professional lives were so deeply involved in the research, our attitude/openness/curiosity towards the participants' responses had a high-intensity gradient. We were open to taking risks and allowing possibilities to emerge (Bozalek 2020), making together and enabling each other to become.

The mutual affective engagement that took place during the performance was the first enabling act of our relationship. Haraway (2016) points out that it is essential in research to engage in *becoming together*, to reconfigure research as a practice of play that is both joyful and risky, where our basic assumptions can be altered entirely.

As shown in the previous section, the activists responded in a highly participatory and empathetic way. The performance affected them, provoking strong reactions – not all positive – and unexpected implications. In particular, the group initially had to express their discomfort at being confronted with such strong emotional content. For example, several activists referred to difficulties in dealing emotionally with the violence depicted (excerpt 1).

The affects of the performance began to be elaborated and used to reflect on the experiences of LGBTQIA+ people as the discussion progressed. Several activists drew connections between Jess's experience and their own. For example, they commented on how Jess's feelings about entering a lesbian bar for the first time were a crucial and shared experience.

Gradually, in the discussion, two main themes of the performance emerged as significant for the group: the topic of *violence* and the *queer community*. The two themes were intertwined within the conversation, echoing each other in co-defining queer reality, sometimes described as violence-driven and sometimes as community-generated.

It was interesting to see how the group collectively developed a common position, transforming the experience of the performance in a collective reflection, not limited to an intellectual response, but engaging affectively in constructing a shared horizon. The group response reaffirmed the need to build small, large, distributed, and socio-material queer communities as "places" to find one's own affirmative space.

With a response-ability tension, the research process promoted what Despret (2008, 2013, 2016) called *rendering each other capable*. It stimulated the activists' reflection on the meaning of the community and their role in promoting a way to "lift up" others, particularly newcomers. It was able to elicit questions that matter to the respondents.

The research showed how, for the activists in the focus group, the queer community is still care, home, chosen family, protection, a place of solidarity, support, and an antidote to violence. Therefore, the community is a safe place where multiple subjectivities can flourish. As pointed out by Bozalek (2020), there is a strong connection between the concept of response-ability and helping life to flourish in the world.

However, the reflection on the importance of community as a place of affirmation emerged because the activists' discussion, fostered in the horizon of response-able research, re-created a community in the focus group at that very moment. Response-able research performed an act of re-grouping, creating the context of a small community in which the subjectivities as LGBTQIA+ activists could flourish. While we, as activists, were commenting on the theme of community, we were becoming a community. We have all affirmed ourselves as queer subjects by rendering each other capable. As Gherardi (2019) points out, practitioners are the effects of the socio-material practices in which they are involved. Therefore, we produce our *becoming activists* because of the encounters with human and nonhuman elements and forces that participated in our meeting.

The response-able research put all the participants in a relational movement that placed us in a joyful and playful danger – open to the unexpected. The discussion changed the participants (including us), creating new atmospheres, intensity fields, movements, gaps, and openings. It was an emotional exchange in which we all were exposed to danger. Still, there was a strong sense of mutual recognition and emotional support enabling response-ability. It was a place of affirmation, as pointed out by Johnston (2016). Rosi Braidotti (2019) talks about affirmative ethics as a collective practice of building social horizons of hope. Ethics enable us to oppose old forms of domination, actively resisting the present through the configuration of new critical and transformative imaginaries.

In the relationship with the community, we *became with* the other activists. For example, as a theatre director, Carmen wondered if the performance had been too violent. She realized the violence was disturbing because the audience had a strong affective connection with an embodied Jess. It was clear that although we are all exposed to more violent portrayals in movies and TV series, the fact that the violence was embodied on stage and directed at our community was particularly moving for everyone. As a result, Carmen decided not to change the first 30 minutes but to include a warning in the play's presentation. She also worked on the rest of the play, trying to bring out a sense of hope and joyful transformation that could compensate for the violence of the first part.

As activists, we thought about violence, community, and what it means to be a queer activist. We reflected on what a Rete Lenford activist said about the fact that violence against not straight people had always been in the world. We recognized that violence had been part of our history as a queer community, and even if we did not suffer it (so much) personally, it had always informed our way of making community. For example, violence against queer people has enacted many grouping processes, as the history, including Stonewall,[3] shows us. Moreover, the discussion with the community made us reflect on the fact that building a healthy queer community includes accounting for forms of violence that we do not personally suffer. Being a queer activist means participating in building a community that uplifts and protects all its members and allows them to become who they want to be.

As researchers, we were changed by the experience. We realized how our activist, artistic, and research subjectivities can only be artificially disentangled. It was our first research experience in the queer community, and we faced some challenges. We felt the discomfort (as the playwright-director and researchers who set up the focus group) of feeling the anger of the participants who were moved by the violent representation. At the same time, we realized the power of the performance as a research trigger, a question posed not only linguistically but performatively through the shared experience of a theatre performance. The performance elicited a response capable of mobilizing affects and penetrating the warmest and most vulnerable area of our LGBTQIA+ subjectivity. Arriving in this zone of high intensity, we tuned into a frequency of kindness to try to *become* – smoothly and without rupture – *with* the activists. This experiment made us appreciate that the ethics of kindness in research is not, or at least not only, a moral duty; it is a necessary quality of listening and attunement, a crucial way of doing response-able research. Without kindness, others cannot open up, and we cannot *become with* them.

Conclusion

With our contribution, we started from a concept of response-ability already present in queer communities and brought it into academic reflection about research practices. We have decentralized the authoritative scientific voice to *become* researchers *with* the queer community, affectively attuning ourselves to queer people. We followed Despret's direction, structuring the research in a performative sense, developing questions that could interest the participants and using a methodology capable of reaffirming the public and aesthetic dimension of the production of scientific knowledge. In the research, we placed ourselves in a dynamic and moving relationship of harmony with the participants. Therefore, we argue with our case that the harmony created between those who attended the performance, tuning into the themes of violence and the role of community, was generating intensity by embodying the affirmative ethics in which our subjectivities were able to express themselves, flourish, and co-become.

To conclude, we agree with Bozalek and Michalinos (2023), who claim that response-ability refers not only to the ability to respond but also to the capacity to enable and invite others' responses. It entails a principle of connection and inseparability embodied in matter (Barad 2017) resulting from human and nonhuman encounters. We experimented with a theatre performance in response-able research practices to investigate queerness. Starting from considering the emergent character of our activities as researchers and activists reflecting on that experience in terms of responsiveness, affect, attunement, and affirmative ethics, we explored theatre performance as a research tool. The focus group's atmosphere was emotionally charged because the activists were touched personally and resonated affectively with the protagonist's feelings. This empathic commonality enabled a safe space where the participants could respond to each other and express their feelings, including anger and fear.

Thus, we claim the art-based focus group enacted forces that stimulated the participants' responses in their affective connection. Playing with the affects mobilized by the performance, the participants (including the researchers) *became together*, developing an empathic commonality where mirroring and recognition processes fostered care and mutual affirmation. Appropriate questions and the availability to be affected by the other – and changing the point of view by empathically including the other – are what enable response-ability in research practices. In this sense, response-ability in research can be conceptualized as affective attunement practiced with politeness, like the politeness taking place in healthy queer communities that enable queer subjectivities to flourish and co-becoming.

Recommended Reading

Original Text by Vinciane Despret and Brett Buchanan

Despret, Vinciane, and Brett Buchanan. 2018. "Animal Abecedary: "O for œuvres" and "Q for queer"." In *The Philosophical Ethology of Vinciane Despret*, 141–156. Routledge.

Key Academic Text

Barad, Karen. "Nature's queer performativity." *Qui Parle: Critical Humanities and Social Sciences* 19, no. 2 (2011): 121–158.

Accessible Resource

Link to the promo of the theatre play "Stone", written and directed by Carmen Pellegrinelli https://www.youtube.com/watch?v=4PDAiuC4nMU&t=1s

Notes

1 Stone is an original theatre play written as a monologue and played by a non-binary actor. The original playscript is freely inspired by one of the narrative lines of the book that resonates more with the personal experiences of the interpreter and the playwriter-director and their knowledge of the queer community. The interpreter Laura M. is a young queer performer who narrates a story by playing several characters. Therefore, the theatre play Stone is not a representation of the book. Instead, it intends to be a narration, a contemporary version of a queer story that belongs to the history of LGBTQIA+ movement culture and questions hegemonic binarism.

2 We acknowledge Barad's non-binary gender self-identification and, hence, we decline verbs accordingly.

3 Stonewall Riot is considered a watershed event that gave rise to the gay liberation movement and the 20th-century fight for LGBTQIA+ rights.

References

Anderson, Ben. 2009. "Affective atmospheres." *Emotion, Space and Society* 2 (2): 77–81.

Barad, Karen. 2007. *Meeting the universe halfway: Quantum physics and the entanglement of matter and meaning.* Duke University Press.

Barad, Karen. 2017. "Troubling time/s and ecologies of nothingness: Re-turning, re-membering, and facing the incalculable." *New Formations* 92 (92): 56–86.

Barad, Karen, and Daniela Gandorfer. 2021. "Political desirings: Yearnings for mattering (,) differently." *Theory & Event* 24 (1): 14–66.

Bozalek, Vivienne. 2020. "Rendering each other capable: Doing response-able research responsibly." In Murris Karin (Ed) *Navigating the postqualitative, new materialist and critical posthumanist terrain across disciplines*, 135–149. Routledge.

Bozalek, Vivienne, and Michalinos Zembylas. 2023. *Responsibility, privileged irresponsibility and response-ability: Higher Education, Coloniality and Ecological Damage*, Springer.

Braidotti, Rosi. 2019. *Posthuman knowledge.* John Wiley & Sons.

Despret, Vinciane. 2008. "The becomings of subjectivity in animal worlds." *Subjectivity* 23: 123–139.

Despret, Vinciane. 2013. "Responding bodies and partial affinities in human–animal worlds." *Theory, Culture & Society* 30 (7–8): 51–76.

Despret, Vinciane. 2016. *What would animals say if we asked the right questions?* Vol. 38. University of Minnesota Press.

Feinberg, Leslie. 1993. *Stone butch blues.* Firebrand Books.

Feinberg, Leslie. 2014. *Stone butch blues.* First Self-Published Edition.

Formby, Eleanor. 2017. *Exploring LGBT spaces and communities: Contrasting identities, belongings and wellbeing.* Taylor & Francis.

Gherardi, Silvia. 2019. *How to conduct a practice-based study: Problems and methods*. Edward Elgar Publishing.

Haraway, Donna. 2015. "Anthropocene, capitalocene, plantationocene, chthulucene: Making Kin." *Environmental Humanities* 6 (1): 159–165.

Haraway, Donna J. 2016. *Staying with the trouble: Making kin in the Chthulucene*. Duke University Press.

Johnston, Tim R. 2016. *Affirmation, care ethics, and LGBT identity*. Springer.

Massumi, Brian. 2015. *Politics of Affect*. Polity.

Pellegrinelli, Carmen, and Parolin Laura Lucia, 2023 "'Alice in Wondertheatre': An affective ethnography." In Cozza, Michela and Gherardi, Silvia (Eds) *The posthumanist epistemology of practice theory: Re-imagining method in organization studies and beyond*, 151–176. Palgrave Macmillan.

Weston, Kath. 1997. *Families we choose: Lesbians, gays, kinship*. Columbia University Press.

Zourabichvili, François. 2012. *Deleuze: A philosophy of the event: Together with the vocabulary of Deleuze*. Edinburgh University Press.

6 Response-able Management-as-Practice

The Ability to Respond

Marcelo de Souza Bispo

Introduction

This chapter aims to open a debate on how management can happen in different ways and move from managerialism to a response-able management-as-practice. It moves away from the idea of management based on (neo)liberalism (Hanlon 2018) by being inspired by a posthuman practice theory (Gherardi 2019, 2021; Gherardi and Laasch 2021), by the ethics of care (Tronto 1993, 2015; Gherardi and Rodeschini 2016) and by the concept of response-ability (Murris and Bozalek 2019; Bozalek 2020).

Managerialism emphasizes rationality, neutrality, technicity and ultra-individualism (Bispo 2022), as well as advocates for achieving efficiency to maximize profits (Parker 2002; Spillane and Jean-Etienne 2023). It is a male perspective rooted in individualism and ethics of justice (Eicher-Catt 2018). A response-able perspective, instead, relies on the ethics of care (Murris and Bozalek 2019; Bozalek 2020). Accordingly, this chapter proposes an alternative management approach focused on care and response-ability.

Although several practitioners and organizations acknowledge the need to implement responsible management, the understanding of how to deal with it changes. For many scholars and practitioners, managerialism is one of the ways to be responsible for society's needs (Parker 2002). From this perspective, the core idea is that "good management" can provide the tools to solve societal issues because "anything that is problematic or chaotic is potentially a target for management" (Parker 2002, 7). However, "good management" based on managerialism was not created to tackle issues, such as poverty, climate change and inequality, although several management scholars and practitioners believe that managerialism can help overcome them.

The mainstream conceptualization of "good management" draws on the idea of efficiency as a reference to all social life aspects (Alexander 2008; Chamayou 2020). From this perspective, "good management" is associated with society's managerialization (Shatil 2020). For Parker (2002, 4), management "is the consolidation of order and efficiency, and who could be against

DOI: 10.4324/9781003452485-6

order and efficiency?" According to this perspective, if society still faces problems, it means we have not achieved the required efficiency level. Efficiency, in this context, is subordinate to market economy ideas (Rodrigues 2013; Jaeggi 2018), according to which both efficiency and profit-making hold moral rule status (Fourcade and Healy 2007).

The efficiency morality underpinning managerialism faces the moral dilemma of how to address societal issues without compromising profit. Corporate discourses pro sustainable, responsible and ethical practices often contradict management practices themselves by distancing what is said from what is done. Unfortunately, corporate scandals are not rare (Surdu 2022), even in companies that define themselves as "responsible." Vale, for example, is a Brazilian organization and one of the biggest mining companies worldwide. It was involved in two dam-collapsing disasters (Brumadinho and Mariana in Brazil) which killed many people and animals, destroyed cities and caused significant environmental and social damage (Darlington et al. 2019). Vale handles its responsibility for these cases from a juridical perspective oriented by the organization's efficiency. The company's financial condition was not significantly affected by these disasters, and, nowadays, its market value is higher than it was before the aforementioned events (Fogaça, Raeder and Marques 2023; Silva and Barros 2023). On the other hand, several stakeholders are not receiving proper assistance from the company; consequently, they are facing some difficulties (Trindade and Bergamo 2024).

Corporate scandals emphasize competing values between the underpinning morality of managerialism and societal needs. More than a technical situation, the relationship between management and societal challenges involves the morality driving management practices. The herein-advocated assumption lies in the fact that we cannot change the current status of things by reproducing the same thinking that brought us here. If society really wants to change toward a more sustainable, responsible and response-able world through management, it is necessary to adopt a new type of management and morality, different from managerialism. Managerialism "is ultimately a form of thought and activity which is being used to justify considerable cruelty and inequality" (Parker 2002, 9).

Morality, in this chapter, is not related to a divine or natural law accounting for expressing standard *a priori* behaviors (theoretical-juridical model) by focusing on how things should be. On the contrary, morality is here conceived as enacted, situated and enmeshed in social life (Walker 2002, 2007).

> [T]heories of morality are attempts to find out what people are doing in bringing moral evaluation to bear (in judgment, feeling, and response) on what they and others do and care about, and whether some ways of doing what they are doing are better ways than others.
>
> (Walker 2007, 16)

The process of assessing management morality highlights conflicting values in society, as well as contradictions in management practices (Abend 2014).

Away from managerialism, the ethics of care can be understood as a viable moral theory (Tronto 1993; Held 2006; Eicher-Catt 2018) to think about management, according to which acknowledging privileges and vulnerabilities (Tronto 2012) opens room for response-able management (Bozalek 2020).

The reason to adopt the idea of "response-able management-as-practice" rather than "responsible management", which is consolidated in the management literature, lies in the fact that responsible management is an umbrella term covering many issues, epistemes and theories about sustainability, corporate social responsibility and business ethics (Laasch et al. 2020). Moreover, according to many practitioners and scholars, the idea of responsible management appears to be anchored in a premise according to which not only it is possible to harmonize financial results' maximization with societal challenges, but social issues are seen as strategic elements for efficiency, itself (e.g., Benjamin and Biswas 2022; Bouslah et al. 2022). This perspective opens room to assess matters associated with greenwashing (Pizzetti, Gatti and Seele 2021), for example. The idea of response-able management-as-practice was herein adopted given the significant number of possibilities covered by the term "responsible management."

The first part of this chapter presents a brief overview of practice-based theories and posthumanism in management studies. Then, it introduces management from the perspective of practice-based theory. Subsequently, it suggests how management-as-practice can be response-able. Finally, it presents some reflections on the importance of grasping the morality of managerialism to propose other management lenses capable of responding to people and organizations. This idea is herein introduced because it is key to the concept of response-ability.

Management from the Perspective of Practice-Based Theory

The concept of social practice is not new in the literature, mainly in the Philosophy and Sociology fields (Hui, Schatzki and Shove 2017). The herein-adopted social practice approach is anchored in the so-called "Practice Turn" (Schatzki 2001), according to which scholars reinterpret the concept of practice rather than relying on classical practice theories (Gherardi 2022). Social practice aims at understanding and explaining social action, order and change (Nicolini 2013). Practice scholars assume social practices as a central element of social life.

The first stage of Practice Turn was around early 21st century, when the idea of practice was to consolidate the movement. Nowadays, it is possible to split practice theories into two main streams (Gherardi 2022). One is called "humanist" and the other "posthumanist." The humanist approach assumes human beings as a primary or exclusive source of agency, whereas the material world is placed outside the practice. The posthumanist approach focuses on overcoming the limits of dualisms that, for example, privilege humans over nonhumans. Posthumanism assumes a relational epistemology (Gherardi 2022) and "the inseparability of ontology, epistemology, and ethics" (Cozza and Gherardi 2023, 56).

Gherardi (2019) defines social practice as a collective knowledgeable doing of humans and nonhumans, as connection-in-action. Practices are a continuous "agencement of elements (bodies, materialities, discourses and knowledges), which achieve agency by being interconnected" (Bispo 2020, 562). Theories of practice assume social orders as procedural and situated, so that any practice is a constant collective becoming. According to Hora (2020, 280),

> The entire understanding of the social order changes with the praxeological approach. For example, the *homo economicus* model explains action by appealing to individual ends, intentions, and interests; social order is then a product of the combination of individual interests. The homo sociologicus model explains action, pointing to collective norms and values, namely the rules that express social normativity; social order is guaranteed by a normative consensus. On the other hand, the novelty of theories of social practices consists in explaining and understanding actions based on the reconstruction of symbolic structures of knowledge, which, at the same time, 'enable' and limit agents to interpret the world in accordance with certain forms, and to behave accordingly. The social order, therefore, does not appear as a product of the conformity of reciprocal normative expectations but as anchored in collective cognitive and symbolic structures, in a 'shared knowledge' that gives rise to a socially shared way of making sense of the world.
>
> (emphasis in original)

The understanding of management as a social practice is anchored in the idea that it is possible carrying out management in different contexts and in ways that are significantly different from the canonical *homo economicus* driving managerialism. Therefore, this chapter proposes to move away from managerialism as a generic technique applicable to any context with a supposedly neutral and disinterested nature (Klikauer 2015).

Management seen as a collective knowledgeable doing (practice) paves the way to take knowledge as an activity (doing) rather than as an object (being). It means that knowledge is not only something that people have cognitively but rather something that they produce together relationally. This epistemological shift invites us to move from "knowledge" to "knowing" (Gherardi 2019). From this perspective, management is not neutral; it is rather socially and historically done and re-done through practices. According to Gherardi

(2022, 102), “the collective activity of knowing takes place in situated practices, and, in practicing, the social and historical knowledgeability of management as a practice domain is performed.”

The passage from knowledge to knowing and the acknowledgment of the importance of socio-historical features for management purposes entails an onto-epistemological change in how we focus on management.

> In moving from the noun to the verb, we also move from issues of ontology (what management *is*) to issues of epistemology (how management is *done*) to issues of onto-epistemology, that is, how the researcher’s language and epistemic practices construct management as an object of inquiry.
>
> (Gherardi 2022, 102)

Understanding management in a situated, processual and relational manner (managing) is key to re-think its morality away from efficiency as a sole principle. Management can value different things (depending on the context) and enact other moralities that are always situated and enmeshed in social life (Walker 2002, 2007). Management conceived as social practice breaks with the idea of neutrality and rationality that rules the management studies field and, furthermore, enables new ways of thinking and doing management (Gherardi and Laasch 2021; Bispo 2022).

Management-as-practice acknowledges that management is processual, relational and changing over time. However, the morality guiding collective action and knowledgeable deeds is an aspect that remains poorly explored in practice theories that may be key to help better understand how practices enact, reproduce and change gradually.

> When moral understandings are ‘shared’ their force in defining responsibilities and prerogatives is recognized in common; this need not mean that they are endorsed by all or exist by the consent of those who live them, nor that all understand the same things about how they are maintained, and who bears their costs or reaps their benefits.
>
> (Walker 2007, 7)

Exploring morality helps a better understanding of social practice dynamics. Most specifically, focusing on management morality helps unveil contradictions in management practices regarding what is said and what is done. It is an opportunity to force a concrete debate about competing priorities in social life.

Response-able Management-as-Practice

Although several critical scholars have highlighted issues concerning managerialism, most management scholars have yet to acknowledge them.

They either neglect or are unaware of managerialism as an ideology causing social problems (Parker 2002, Dardot and Laval 2016; Chamayou 2020). It does not happen because these people are inherently bad and because they share a morality that prevents them from seeing how to do management differently by adopting a different morality. It happens because "makes knowledge in and of morality [is] thoroughly enmeshed with social knowledge, both articulate and implicit" (Walker 2007, 4).

Understanding these premises is key to introduce the concept of response-able management from a practice-based perspective, which looks at what people do rather than what they say they do. This is the reason why it is important to present and explain morality associated with the ideology of managerialism as the first step toward a "response-able management-as-practice."

The idea that efficiency and responsibility can work together is widely discussed in the academic literature with several scholars believing that the market is the key to achieving this balance (Polanyi 1980; Callon 1998; Ganem 2012). According to this view, economic principles focused on productivity, as well as morals of justice and social responsibility (Fourcade and Healy 2007), can all be addressed through the market. Klikauer (2015) advocates that the traditional triple-bottom-line concept, which includes environmental, economic and social factors, should be reframed as people, planet and profit. Therefore, profit always appears as a priority, although, most of the time, the word "profit" is replaced by others, such as efficiency, development, (financial) sustainability and fairness.

It is important to emphasize that social demands are often seen as secondary in profit-driven societies and that responsible actions are only taken if they do not hinder the maximization of financial results (Bispo 2022). However, it is essential to highlight that it is not a choice between profit and loss or a matter of responsibility or irresponsibility. Focusing solely on maximizing financial results as the primary goal can limit considerations about other valuable aspects, mainly when resources are limited.

Despite the discourse on corporate social responsibility, sustainability and business ethics (Hibbert and Cunliffe 2015; Klikauer 2015; Rasche and Gilbert 2015; Rhodes and Fleming 2020), managerialism oriented to maximizing profits does not open room to see collective demands through other lenses because of its individualistic and hierarchical feature, which privileges few to the detriment of the majority, under the justification of meritocracy. This managerial logic is not restricted to corporate organizations, but it becomes a model for public institutions, non-governmental organizations and social life (Dardot and Laval 2016; Chamayou 2020). It is an entire society that becomes subject to market rules (Fourcade and Healy 2007).

An alternative morality is necessary to overcome the current scenario because the paradox of responsible management has efficiency as its moral paradigm.

I draw on the ethics of care as a viable moral theory (Tronto 2012), which differs from the justice/rights perspective underpinning managerialism (Eicher-Catt 2018).

> An ethic of justice focuses on questions of fairness, equality, individual rights, abstract principles, and the consistent application of them. An ethic of care focuses on attentiveness, trust, responsiveness to need, narrative nuance, and cultivating caring relations. Whereas an ethic of justice seeks a fair solution between competing individual interests and rights, an ethic of care sees the interests of carers and cared-for as importantly intertwined rather than as simply competing. Whereas justice protects equality and freedom, care fosters social bonds and cooperation.
>
> (Held 2006, 15)

The ethics of justice asks, "What is just?", whereas the ethics of care asks, "How to respond?" (Held 2006). The term "care" used as a noun is associated with values and it concerns the moral order, good and bad. On the other hand, "caring" used as a verb is associated with practices involved in providing care and with how its value is determined in practice. Caring is a practice involving the collective capacity to take care of and for someone. It is a continuous, adaptable and open-ended response to the needs of those being cared for (Gherardi and Rodeschini 2016). According to Held (2006, 10; emphasis in original),

> the central focus of the ethics of care is on the compelling moral salience of attending to and meeting the needs of the particular others for whom we take responsibility. [...] The ethics of care attends to this central concern of human life and delineates the moral values involved. It refuses to relegate care to a realm 'outside morality'.

Care is both value and practice; care seen as practice (caring) implies that it is simultaneously thought and action, in a way that both are closely linked and oriented to a particular end (Held 2006; Spinelli 2022). Following Tronto (1993, 2012, 2015) who encourages scholars to focus on the moral boundaries that preclude elevating ethics of care to the status of a full-fledged moral and political theory, I propose using the ethics of care to reshape how to think about management in terms of response-able management-as-practice.

> Many people believe that an ethic of care cannot provide a sufficiently broad or robust moral justification for considering global questions. I have suggested here that an account of relational responsibility can help us to move forward by asking citizens to begin the hard work of assessing their values and relationships, that is, by asking what they care about, what they must care for, how they must give care and respond to care-giving

> practices. To recognize how fundamental are our relationships of care requires a thoroughgoing rethinking of political life.
>
> (Tronto 2012, 314)

Response-able management-as-practice grounds moral decision-making in a situated space and it is contextually supported by concrete lived experience. It should be contextually theorized as relational ethics bond to one's position in society (Eicher-Catt 2018). "Management practices are not only concerned with what managers 'do,' but also with the consequences of their 'doings,' and thus responsible managing is inscribed within situated practices of responsibility, sustainability, and ethics" (Gherardi 2021, 6, emphasis in original).

Tronto (2012, 309) points out that a "relational account of responsibility is better because it places conflicts about responsibility at the core of every individual and institution's political, social, and epistemological orientation."

Response-able management-as-practice is a texture of caring practices (Price, Gherardi and Manidis 2020) fostering social bonds and cooperation. This feature is more important where vulnerable social conditions are more evident. Different from Gherardi and Laasch (2021), who have diminished the effects of capitalism to explain and understand responsible management practices, I advocate that it is not possible to overlook tensions and conflicts triggered by market rules oriented by the capitalist assumption of accumulation in countries and places where capitalism effects are more cruel and evident through inequalities.

Theorizing responsible management from the perspective of the Global South forces researchers to look at the effects of capitalism and colonization to understand responsibility and response-ability. Theories of practice often highlight the situatedness and historical features of practices. However, they overlook the historical process produced by both capitalism and colonization worldwide (Ibarra-Colado 2006), and hence, it demands an accurate analysis of conflicts and tensions from the Global South perspective. Response-able management-as-practice research response-ably invites us to acknowledge rather than erase the history of scientific knowledge-making practices over the centuries, as well as to appreciate how inequalities produced so far affect the way researchers theorize social phenomena.

Conclusion

This chapter aimed to open a debate on how management can be performed differently, by moving from managerialism to response-able management-as-practice. It is essential to deepen the understanding of what contemporary management is, what it is for and how actors collaborate to sustain and justify the current morality. It is important to grasp the values supporting the dominant ideology and the moral basis of management to better understand that management rationality, technicality and neutrality are driven by the neoliberal view according to which the (financial) market works as an efficiency model to all social life aspects. Replacing the idea of efficiency with that of caring and response-ability enables acknowledging that the harmony among profit maximization, sustainability and responsibility is unviable. Responsible management requires another morality type.

I believe that it is possible to create a new type of management capable of working toward more response-able practices. Management studies have generated valuable knowledge to help us organize processes, avoid waste, properly manage financial resources and find more sustainable solutions. This knowledge should be rooted in moral principles of caring for both the planet and its inhabitants (humans and nonhumans) rather than serving the interests of a few (humans) at the expense of many (other humans and nonhumans). By doing so, management can concretely contribute to response-able practices. By proposing a fresh perspective on what can be understood as management based on the idea of response-able management-as-practice, I emphasize management's ability to respond differently to significant societal challenges, such as climate change, inequalities and poverty. Response-able management-as-practice moves from the individualistic understanding of responsibility to that of response-ability to render each other capable of responding (Bozalek 2020). Responsible and response-able practices have the potential to educate people (Bispo 2022) toward a different thinking and doing in their professional and private lives, by not resuming life to a business. Finally, the concept of response-ability can open room for decolonizing research and theory besides bringing different understandings of social practices and management.

Recommended Reading

Original Text by Joan Tronto

Tronto, Joan C. 2010. "Creating Caring Institutions: Politics, Plurality, and Purpose." *Ethics and Social Welfare* 4 (2): 158–171. https://doi.org/10.1080/17496535.2010.484259.

Key Academic Text

Shepherd, Sue. 2017. "Managerialism: An Ideal Type." *Studies in Higher Education* 43, no. 9: 1668–1678. https://doi.org/10.1080/03075079.2017.1281239.

Accessible Resource

Bispo, Marcelo, "Educational Practice with Sylvia Gherardi and Ted Schatzki," YouTube vídeo, 42:28, January 1, 2024, https://www.youtube.com/watch?app=desktop&v=CbPZ166ZXbE

References

Abend, Gabriel. 2014. *The Moral Background: An Inquiry into the History of Business Ethics*. Princeton: Princeton University Press.

Alexander, Jennifer Karns. 2008. *The Mantra of Efficiency: From Waterwheel to Social Control*. Baltimore: JHU Press.

Benjamin, Samuel Jebaraj, and Pallab Kumar Biswas. 2022. "Does Winning a CSR Award Increase Firm Value?" *International Journal of Disclosure and Governance*, 19, no. 3: 313–329.

Bispo, Marcelo. 2013. "Estudos Baseados Em Prática: Conceitos, História E Perspectivas." *Revista Interdisciplinar De Gestão Social*, 2, no. 1. https://doi.org/10.9771/23172428rigs.v2i1.10058.

Bispo, Marcelo. 2020. "Book Review: Silvia Gherardi's Influence on Practice-Based Studies and Organizational Research." *Qualitative Research in Organizations and Management: An International Journal*, 15, no. 4: 561–565.

Bispo, Marcelo. 2022. "Responsible Managing as Educational Practice." *Organization Management Journal*, 19, no. 4: 155–166. https://doi.org/10.1108/QROM-11-2019-1857

Bouslah, Kais, Abdelmajid Hmaittane, Lawrence Kryzanowski, and Bouchra M'Zali. 2023. "CSR Structures: Evidence, Drivers, and Firm Value Implications." *Journal of Business Ethics*, 185, no. 1: 115–145.

Bozalek, Vivienne. 2020. "Rendering Each Other Capable: Doing Response-able Research Responsibly." In *Navigating the Postqualitative, New Materialist and Critical Posthumanist Terrain Across Disciplines*, edited by Karin Murris, 135–149. London: Routledge.

Callon, Michel. 1998. *The Law of the Markets*. Oxford: Blackwell.

Chamayou, Gregoire. 2020. *A sociedade ingovernável: uma genealogia do liberalismo autoritário*. São Paulo: Ubu Editora.

Cozza, Michela, and Silvia Gherardi. 2023. "Chapter 4: Posthuman Feminism and Feminist New Materialism: Towards an Ethico-onto-Epistemology in Research Practices." In *Handbook of feminist research methodologies in management and organization studies*. Cheltenham: Edward Elgar Publishing, accessed Jan 31, 2024, https://doi.org/10.4337/9781800377035.00011

Dardot, Pierre, and Christian Laval. 2016. *A nova razão do mundo: ensaio sobre a sociedade neoliberal*. São Paulo: Editora Boitempo.

Darlington, Glanz, Andreoni Bloch, and Peçanha Singhvi. 2019, February 9. *Brumadinho Dam Collapse: A Tidal Wave of Mud*. The New York Times Company. Retrieved from https://www.nytimes.com/interactive/2019/02/09/world/americas/brazil-dam-collapse.html

Eicher-Catt, Debora. 2018. "Joan C. Tronto: Ethic of Care Across Boundaries." In *An Encyclopedia of Communication Ethics: Goods in Contention*, edited by Ronald C. Arnett, Annette M. Holba, and Susan Mancino, 494–498. New York: Peter Lang.

Fogaça, Pedro Augusto, Francisco Teixeira Raeder, and José Augusto Veiga da Costa Marques. 2023. "AnáLise Dos Impactos Dos Acidentes Ambientais de Mariana e Brumadinho Nas AçõEs Da Mineradora Vale." *Reunir: Revista de Administração, Ciências Contábeis e Sustentabilidade*, 13, no. 2: 1–18.

Fourcade, Marion, and Kieran Healy. 2007. "Moral Views of Market Society." *Annual Review of Sociology*, 33, no. 1: 285–311.

Ganem, Angela. 2012. "O mercado como ordem social em Adam Smith, Walras e Hayek." *Economia e Sociedade*, 21, no. 1: 143–164.

Gherardi, Silvia. 2019. *How to Conduct a Practice-Based Study*. 2nd ed. Cheltenham: Elgar Publishing.

Gherardi, Silvia. 2022. "A Posthumanist Epistemology of Practice." In *Handbook of Philosophy of Management. Handbooks in Philosophy*, edited by Cristina Neesham, Markus Reihlen, and Dennis Schoeneborn, 99–120. Switzerland: Springer. https://doi.org/10.1007/978-3-319-48352-8_53-1.

Gherardi, Silvia, and Giulia Rodeschini. 2016. "Caring as a Collective Knowledgeable Doing: About Concern and Being Concerned." *Management Learning*, 47, no. 3: 266–284. https://doi.org/10.1177/1350507615610030.

Gherardi, Silvia, and Oliver Laasch. 2021. "Responsible Management-as-Practice: Mobilizing a Posthumanist Approach." *Journal of Business Ethics*. https://doi.org/10.1007/s10551-021-04945-7.

Hanlon, Gerard. 2018. "The First Neo-Liberal Science: Management and Neo-Liberalism." *Sociology*, 52, no. 2: 298–315. https://doi.org/10.1177/0038038516655260.

Held, Virginia. 2006. *Ethics of Care: Personal, Political, and Global*. Oxford: Oxford University Press.

Hora, Leonardo. 2020. "Capitalismo como prática social?: os potenciais e desafios de uma aproximação entre o practice turn em teoria social e a interpretação do capitalismo." *Trans/Form/Ação*, 43, no. 3: 277–302. https://doi.org/10.1590/0101-3173.2020.v43n3.20.p277

Ibarra-Colado, Eduardo. 2006. "Organization Studies and Epistemic Coloniality in Latin America: Thinking Otherness from the Margins." *Organization*, 13, no. 4: 463–488. https://doi.org/10.1177/1350508406065851

Jaeggi, Rahel. 2018. "Um conceito amplo de economia." *Civitas*, 18, no. 3: 503–522. https://doi.org/10.15448/1984-7289.2018.3.32368

Klikauer, Thomas. 2015. "What Is Managerialism?" *Critical Sociology*, 41, no. 7–8: 1103–1119. https://doi.org/10.1177/0896920513501351.

Murris, Karin, and Vivienne Bozalek. 2019. "Diffraction and Response-able Reading of Texts: The Relational Ontologies of Barad and Deleuze." *International Journal of Qualitative Studies in Education*, 32, no. 7: 872–886. https://doi.org/10.1080/09518398.2019.1609122

Nicolini, Davide. 2013. *Practice Theory, Work, & Organization: An Introduction*. Oxford: Oxford University Press.

Parker, Martin. 2002. *Against Management: Organization in the Age of Managerialism*. Cambridge: Polity Press.

Pizzetti, Marta, Lucia Gatti, and Peter Seele. 2021. "Firms Talk, Suppliers Walk: Analyzing the Locus of Greenwashing in the Blame Game and Introducing 'Vicarious Greenwashing'." *Journal of Business Ethics*, 170, no. 1: 21–38.

Polanyi, Karl. 1980. *A grande Transformação: as origens de nossa época*. Rio de Janeiro: Campus.

Price, Oriana Milani, Silvia Gherardi, and Marie Manidis. 2020. "Enacting Responsible Management: A Practice-Based Perspective." In: *The Research Handbook of Responsible Management*, edited by Oliver Laasch, Roy Suddaby, R. Edward Freeman, and Dima Jamali, 392–409. Cheltenham: Edward Elgar. https://doi.org/10.4337/9781788971966.00035.

Rasch, Andreas and Dirk Ulrich Gilbert. 2015. "Decoupling Responsible Management Education: Why Business Schools May Not Walk Their Talk." *Journal of Management Inquiry*, 24, no. 3: 239–252. https://doi.org/10.1177/1056492614567315.

Rhodes, Carl, and Peter Fleming. 2020. "Forget Political Corporate Social Responsibility." *Organization*, 27, no. 6: 943–951. https://doi.org/10.1177/1350508420928526.

Rodrigues, João. 2013. "The Political and Moral Economies of Neoliberalism: Mises and Hayek." *Cambridge Journal of Economics*, 37: 1001–1017.

Schatzki, Theodore Richard. 2001. "Introduction: Practice Theory." In: *The Practice Turn in Contemporary Theory*, edited by Theodore Richard Schatzki, Karin Knorr Cetina, and Eike von Savigny, 1–14. New York: Routledge.

Shatil, Sharron. 2020. "Managerialism – A Social Order on the Rise." *Critical Sociology*, 46, no. 7–8: 1189–1206. https://doi.org/10.1177/0896920520911703.

Silva, Rita C., and Cláudio M. E. Barros. 2023. "Acidente de Brumadinho em Minas Gerais: Valoração das ações da Vale S.A. e Seus Pares." *Revista Mineira de Contabilidade*, 24, no. 3: 40–50.

Spillane, Robert, and Jean-Etienne Joullié. 2023. "The Decline of Authority and the Rise of Managerialism." *Organization*, 30, no. 5: 961–980. https://doi.org/10.1177/13505084211061242.

Spinelli, Letícia. 2022. "Joan Tronto: Responsabilidade relacional, reconhecimento de privilégios e vulnerabilidade." *Princípios: Revista de Filosofia*, 29, no. 58, 63–83. https://doi.org/10.21680/1983-2109.2022v29n58ID23774.

Surdu, Irina. 2022. "Why Big Firms Are Rarely Toppled by Corporate Scandals – New Research." *The Conversation*, March 10, 2022. https://theconversation.com/why-big-firms-are-rarely-toppled-by-corporate-scandals-new-research-176270.

Trindade, Eliane, and Marlene Bergamo. 2024. "After 5 Years, Brumadinho Deals with Dependence on the 'Tragedy Fund'." *Folha de São Paulo*, January 11, 2024. https://folha.com/c4yfhite

Tronto, Joan. 1993. *Moral Boundaries. A Political Argument for an Ethic of Care*. New York: Routledge.

Tronto, Joan. 2012. "Partiality Based on Relational Responsibilities: Another Approach to Global Ethics." *Ethics and Social Welfare*, 6, no. 3: 303–316. https://doi.org/10.1080/17496535.2012.704058.

Tronto, Joan. 2015. *Who Cares? How to Reshape a Democratic Politics*. New York: Cornell University Press.

Walker, Margaret U. 2002. "Morality in Practice: A Response to Claudia Card and Lorraine Code." *Hypatia*, 17, no. 1: 174–182.

Walker, Margaret. 2007. *Moral Understandings: A Feminist Study in Ethics* (2nd ed.). Oxford: University Press.

Index

Note: Page numbers followed by "n" denote endnotes.

For Product Safety Concerns and Information please contact our EU representative GPSR@taylorandfrancis.com
Taylor & Francis Verlag GmbH, Kaufingerstraße 24, 80331 München, Germany

www.ingramcontent.com/pod-product-compliance
Lightning Source LLC
LaVergne TN
LVHW010938110826
845149LV00013B/2654

* 9 7 8 1 0 3 2 5 8 9 9 1 6 *